Contents

Don't Pee In The Gym Shower

Common Sense Manners and Etiquette
For The Common Senseless

Nicholas Kilburn

Chapter One

Forward

Writing this book has been a passion project of mine for many years. So many of the lessons and rules I discuss in the book took me decades to learn. Only in my twenties did I learn that offering gas money to a friend who drove me was considerate. I have lost count on how many times I was invited to someone's home for dinner and I came empty-handed. Not knowing how to make small talk; which topics were safe to bring up and which were taboo from speaking about. I had always thought that I grew up knowing how to handle myself in any situation that may arise, but once I became an adult and experienced the real world, I was shocked and saddened by how less prepared I was. I was missing a key foundation that was never fully taught to me: manners and etiquette. To this day, remembering my teens and early adulthood, I am mortified and dejected that I did not have this foundation in my life. It has undeniably made my life harder and made me feel more secluded from others. Overcoming this has been both a huge endeavor and one of my biggest accomplishments.

A lot of the foundations for manners and etiquette boil down to simple common sense. Many of the basic principles and behaviors associated with good manners and etiquette are rooted in practicality and consideration for others. Common sense mandates we say "please" and "thank you," hold the door for someone, or remain quiet in a serene setting. These are actions that promote respect, kindness, and harmony in our interactions with others. By applying common sense to our social interactions, we can navigate various situations with grace and thoughtfulness, enhancing our relationships and making the world a more pleasant place to be.

My lack of having that foundation has made my social interactions stressful and unenjoyable. Instead of allowing myself to experience the moment and have an enjoyable time with others, I felt out of place, less than, and felt like I was being judged. Someone who goes through it enough times will shy away and back out on being sociable, which may lead to not being able to make friends, network for work, or possibly meet the man or woman of your dreams. The expression "The world is your oyster" feels ironic when your world has become as small as an oyster.

One thing I hope to do with *Don't Pee In The Gym Shower* is address the importance of manners, etiquette, and chivalry in a commonsense way. I see examples every day of people not even realizing that what they are doing or saying shows a lack of awareness, and how it affects not them and others, but other people's perception and opinion of them.

Without having and using this foundation in our daily lives, we lose the things that are essential to us as people: kindness, respect, being sociable, and being valued. From the ever-expanding possibilities of technology to the way it simultaneously connects and distances us, its impact on our social interactions is undeniable. It has opened up new avenues for communication and allowed us to explore previously uncharted territories, while also creating a sense of detachment in our personal connections. Moreover, technology's role in professional settings cannot be ignored. It serves as a powerful tool for networking, attracting potential clients, and gaining recognition from superiors. Embracing and understanding the influence of technology is crucial in navigating the modern landscape of social and professional interactions. From going to formal dinners to hosting your own, I will cover many situations that will require a solid foundation to show your knowledge and execution of manners and etiquette, as well as being as chivalrous as any gentleman or lady should be. By being mindful of these rules, you can elevate any social situation and make a positive impression on those around you.

Are you ready to elevate your social skills and make a lasting impression on those around you? Are you ready to master the art of manners, etiquette, and chivalry to build strong relationships and connections? This book is your guide to becoming the best version of yourself and making positive changes in your personal and professional life. So, are you ready to dive in and start making a difference?

Nicholas Kilburn
29 May, 2023

Chapter Two

Introduction

In today's fast-paced and digital world, it's very easy to get caught up in the hustle and bustle of life, and forget not only about the importance of human connection, but how we interact with one another. We are in a time where technology has dominated our lives, and social interactions have been limited to online messaging, "likes", and emojis. The rapid growth of technology and social media has created a society that is more disconnected and impersonal than ever before. People are more likely to communicate through screens than in person, leading to a decline in face-to-face interactions and a decrease in the importance of social skills, such as good manners and etiquette. We care more about the number of followers we have instead of focusing on the people in our lives and those we meet along the way. As a result, manners and social skills have dissipated. But it's not just technology that's at fault. Manners, etiquette, and chivalry have been on the decline for decades.

Over the past few decades, there has been a noticeable decline in the practice of manners, etiquette, and acts of chivalry. This decline is because of a variety of factors, but primarily the alteration in values and priorities in modern society.

In the past, families and communities held manners, etiquette, and acts of chivalry in the utmost regard. Parents placed a strong emphasis on teaching their children to be respectful, and these values were reinforced in schools and other social institutions. However, in recent years, there has been a shift towards individualism and self-expression, leading to a decline in the importance placed on these traditional values. These values are often seen as antiquated or outdated, and are not always considered relevant in a society that places a high value on individual freedom and self-expression.

This shift towards individualism and self-expression has also led to a decline in social cohesion and community values. People are less likely to feel a sense of responsibility towards their community or society and focused on their own individual needs and desires. This has resulted in a decline in the practice of polite behavior, which is based on the idea of showing respect and consideration towards others.

Another factor contributing to the decline of manners and etiquette is the rise of a consumer culture, where people are encouraged to focus on their own desires and instant gratification. This has led to a decline in patience, self-control, and delayed gratification, which are all key aspects of good manners and etiquette.

However, it is important to note that the shift towards individualism and self-expression is not inherently bad. These values have led to significant progress in areas like civil rights, gender equality, and social justice. However, it is important to find a balance between individual freedom and social responsibility, and to recognize traditional values as manners, etiquette, and chivalry in creating a respectful society.

Another factor contributing to the decline in social graces is the growing influence of popular culture. Many modern TV shows, movies, and music promote rude and disrespectful behavior as being cool or funny, leading to a normalization of impolite behavior.

Whether it's calling women "bitches" and "hos" in many hip-hop and rap songs, celebrity chef Gordon Ramsey on *Hell's Kitchen* going ballistic on contestants and diners alike, or the cute-looking, but foul-mouthed and offensive bear from the self-titled movie *Ted*, teens and young adults are being influenced by what they see and hear. Sadly, a lot of entertainment being made today lacks role models that exhibit respectable behavior that impressionable people can benefit from.

However, the decline in manners, etiquette, and chivalry is not inevitable. By recognizing how important these traditional values are and practicing them in our daily lives, we can work to reverse this trend. Parents can attempt to teach their children manners and respect, schools can reintroduce lessons on etiquette and chivalry, and individuals can attempt to be more polite in their interactions with others.

Businesses can play a role in promoting proper protocol in the workplace by setting standards for professional behavior and training employees on proper workplace etiquette. As a society, we must recognize the value of good manners and etiquette, and attempt to promote and practice these values in all aspects of our lives.

Improving our social skills can have a profound impact on our personal and professional lives. For millennials, in particular, investing in their social skills can pay off in a big way. As the first generation to grow up with smartphones and social media, many millennials may struggle with face-to-face communication and social interactions. By focusing on improving their social skills, they can not only become more confident and effective communicators but also build stronger relationships, both personally and professionally.

But social skills aren't just important for millennials - they're important for everyone. In a world where we are bombarded with digital distractions, taking the time to connect with others on a personal level can be a refreshing change of pace. Good manners and etiquette can help us navigate social situations with grace and ease, while chivalry can remind us of how important treating others with respect and consideration can be.

Ultimately, improving our social skills is about more than just being polite - it's about building deeper, more meaningful connections with the surrounding people, and creating a more empathetic society. So whether you're a millennial looking to boost your career prospects, or just someone who wants to be a little more considerate in their daily interactions, investing in your social skills is a smart and worthwhile endeavor.

As the saying goes, "Manners maketh man" - and for me, that sentiment couldn't be more true. I was raised by a mother who didn't instill in me that manners and etiquette, these traditional social values, need to be a cornerstone of my personal philosophy. It has made my life harder not having this as a part of my developmental growth..

But as I've grown older and more experienced, I have observed the world around me, and noticed a troubling trend: a decline in the importance placed on manners, etiquette, and chivalry in modern society. From rudeness and disrespect in everyday interactions, to the erosion of basic social graces, the values that I hold so dear are in danger of being lost. So, I am determined to do something about it.

With this book, I aim to inspire a renewed appreciation for the importance of good manners, chivalry, and etiquette, and to encourage readers to embody these values in their daily lives Based on my own experiences, as well as the wisdom of experts, and everyday people who embody these values, I will offer a convincing case for why we need to make manners and etiquette a priority again.

This is more than just a nostalgic yearning for a bygone era. My mission is to show that these are timeless values that are just as relevant today as they ever were. By promoting these values and encouraging others to embrace them, I hope to inspire a shift towards a more considerate, kind, respectful, and connected society - one where good manners and etiquette are not just a nicety, but a necessity.

This book on manners is a comprehensive guide to navigating the social world with confidence and grace. You can use it in two ways: first, you can read it from cover to cover to gain a deeper understanding of the principles of good manners and etiquette. The book is organized in a logical and easy-to-follow manner, with each section building upon the previous one. Alternatively, you can turn to the section that interests you the most or the one you need a quick refresher on. Whether you are looking to polish your social skills for personal or professional reasons, this book has everything you need to know to become a well-mannered and respected individual. From mastering the art of small talk to handle tricky situations with ease, this book will equip you with the tools and knowledge needed to succeed in any social setting.

A quick side note before we get started.

Throughout this book, you may notice that there are a few rules, guides, and suggestions that are repeated across different sections and scenarios. This is because the basic principles of good manners and etiquette are universal and can apply to various situations. Whether it is at work, a social gathering, or a formal event, certain behaviors and actions are always considered polite and respectful. By repeating these core principles and practices, we hope to instill a sense of consistency and familiarity that can help you navigate different situations with ease and confidence. Repetition can help reinforce good habits and make them second nature, so that you don't have to think too hard about what to do in a particular situation.

Chapter Three

The Basics: Manners and Etiquette 101

Most people confuse manners and etiquette, but they are not the same thing. The confusion between the two arises from the fact that we often see good manners as an essential part of following etiquette. We regard people who exhibit good manners as well-mannered and more probable to be perceived as socially adept. In contrast, we often view a person who lacks manners as rude or uncivilized.

The societal norms surrounding manners and etiquette are constantly evolving. As a result, people may use the terms interchangeably because what makes up good manners and proper etiquette may vary from culture to culture or even from generation to generation.

In modern times, the increasing emphasis on individualism and self-expression has also contributed to the blurring of the lines between manners and etiquette. This has led to a decline in the importance placed on traditional values such as etiquette and manners, making it more challenging for people to understand the difference between the two.

However, it is essential to understand that etiquette and manners are distinct concepts that play vital roles in social interactions. By recognizing and practicing good manners and proper etiquette, individuals can foster positive interactions with others and build stronger relationships.

Are you unsure about the differences between manners and etiquette? Take this short quiz to test your knowledge and see how much you know about these important social skills. Answer each question to the best of your ability and see how you stack up. Answers will be at the end of this chapter.

Manners or Etiquette?

1. Using a napkin on your lap during a meal?

2. Properly introducing yourself to someone new?

3. Offering your seat to an elderly or pregnant person on public transportation?

4. Knowing which fork to use during a formal meal?

5. Sending a thank-you note after receiving a gift?

6. Saying "excuse me" when passing someone in a crowded space?

7. Knowing when to use formal titles (e.g. Mr., Ms., Dr.) in professional settings?

8. Addressing someone by their preferred pronouns?

9. Waiting for your turn to speak in a group conversation?

10. RSVP'ing to a party invitation in a timely manner?

11. Writing a sympathy card for someone who has experienced a loss?

12. Not using your phone during a meal with others?

13. Being on time for a meeting or appointment?

14. When someone sends you a text message, is it an example of manners or etiquette to respond within a certain amount of time?

15. When you're playing an online multiplayer video game, is it an example of manners or etiquette to not use profanity in chat?

16. When you're walking down the street with a group of friends, is it an example of manners or etiquette to walk on the outside of the sidewalk closest to the road?

17. When you're at a concert or show, is it an example of manners or etiquette to not record the performance on your phone?

18. When you're in a conversation with someone, is it an example of manners or etiquette to not look at your phone or other distractions?

19. When you're in a group chat, is it an example of manners or etiquette to not ignore someone's message or leave them on read?

20. When you're on a date, is it an example of manners or etiquette to not be on your phone or use it excessively?

***

What's The Difference Between Etiquette and Manners?

I love to watch people. I always have. I have always been interested in seeing what other people are doing. My mother used to say that I always had a hard time being put down to sleep when I was a toddler, because I was so curious about what others were doing. I was a curious kid, and I didn't want to miss anything. As I have gotten older, it's still true. I always want to know what's going on. But now, there has been a new thing that has caught my interest, and I must admit, it's a bit of an obsession of mine. It's a major reason I wrote this book.

As I navigate through my daily routine of running errands, working out, and being at the office, I can't help but notice the lack of common courtesy and good manners exhibited by people around me. It seems to be a widespread issue, yet one that is rarely acknowledged or addressed.

People walking down sidewalks or hallways with their heads down staring at their phones, oblivious to their surroundings, doors not being held open for another person, rude and discourteous behavior to people in the service industries. The list seems endless, and with how fast society is changing, with technology making us more and more isolated from each other, it feels like we are losing the last bits of values we have that help bind us all together.

So, what can we do about this dilemma? Turns out, there is a lot we can do, which I will cover throughout this book. Let's take a moment and look at what these values are and how we can define them.

Etiquette and manners are often used interchangeably, but they actually have distinct differences. Etiquette is a set of specific rules and codes of behavior that dictate how one should conduct themselves in social situations. It encompasses a wider scope of behavior than manners, which are more focused on basic courtesies. As an example of etiquette, knowing which fork to use at a formal dining setting or dressing appropriately for a specific occasion, such as wearing a suit when attending a wedding or funeral.

While we often consider etiquette the more sophisticated of the two, it is important to note that it relies on a foundation of good manners. Without basic manners, it is difficult to adhere to proper etiquette. Unlike manners, we must learn etiquette through a conscious effort to understand and practice the specific codes of behavior.

In short, while manners are a crucial starting point for positive social interactions, etiquette takes it a step further by providing a specific set of guidelines for behavior in various social situations.

People commonly refer to polite behavior as manners, which are a set of general behaviors taught to children by parents and schools from an early age. This shows the significant value placed on good manners within society. As children grow, they internalize these behaviors, making them a natural part of their character. Examples of manners include saying 'Thank you' after receiving something, using 'please' when requesting something, apologizing when someone's hurt, and showing respect towards elders.

When a person displays good manners, we perceive them as being well-raised. This emphasizes that manners and etiquette are distinct from each other and refer to different aspects of behavior.

***

How Have Manners and Etiquette Evolved?

The concern for appropriate codes of behavior has existed for thousands of years.

The Maxims of Ptahhotep (around 2375–2350 BCE) is an ancient Egyptian literary composition that dates back to the Old Kingdom era. It is considered being one of the earliest examples of a written code of conduct or etiquette. *The Maxims of Ptahhotep* is a collection of ethical teachings and principles attributed to Ptahhotep, a vizier (high ranking political advisor) to the pharaoh, which were intended to guide people's behavior and attitudes in everyday life. The maxims cover a wide range of topics, including the importance of humility, respect for authority, honesty, generosity, and kindness towards others. They also emphasize the need for wisdom, education, and good judgment in decision-making.

Confucius (551-479 BC) contributed greatly to the development of etiquette and social behavior in China. He emphasized the importance of proper conduct and respect for others in his teachings, known as Confucianism. Confucius believed that the principles of benevolence, righteousness, respect, wisdom, and faithfulness should guide a person's behavior. His teachings focused on the importance of respect for elders, proper communication, and social harmony. The principles of Confucianism greatly influenced the development of Chinese culture and society, including its etiquette practices.

We also know the ancient Greeks have contributed to the development of etiquette. For example, the philosopher Aristotle wrote about the importance of good manners and social behavior in his work, *Nicomachean Ethics*. The Greeks also held feasts and banquets, which required certain rules of behavior, such as the proper way to recline on a couch, how to serve and eat food, and how to engage in conversation with others. These customs and rules helped shape the development of Western etiquette.

The Book of the Courtier, written by Baldassare Castiglione in the 16th century, was a highly influential work and had a significant impact on the development of manners and etiquette in Europe. It was written as a guide for young courtiers in the court of Urbino, Italy, and aimed to teach them how to behave in the courtly society of the time.

The book laid out a set of guidelines for behavior, including advice on dress, conversation, and social interaction. It stressed the importance of grace, charm, and courtesy, as well as the need to be well-educated and knowledgeable about the arts and sciences.

The Book of the Courtier also emphasized the idea of *sprezzatura*, or effortless grace, which meant that one's manners and behavior should appear natural and effortless, even if they required conscious effort to achieve.

Louis XIV, the King of France from 1643 to 1715, is credited with formalizing the rules of etiquette and manners at his court. He established strict rules of conduct for his courtiers and created a complex system of hierarchy and protocol. He introduced the concept of "le Roi Soleil," or "the Sun King," which positioned himself as the center of French cultural and social life. Louis XIV was known for his extravagant court ceremonies, such as the lever and coucher, where he was attended to by his courtiers in a highly structured manner. He also emphasized the importance of dress codes and encouraged his courtiers to wear elaborate and expensive clothing, which further reinforced social distinctions. Louis XIV's contribution to etiquette and manners had a lasting impact on European court culture and social behavior, and we still follow many of his rules and customs in some form today.

Even in the pre and post Revolutionary War era in America, manners were important to the future Founding Fathers. A 14 years old George Washington wrote out a copy from his schoolbook, *The 110 Rules of Civility*. Ben Franklin's popular, *Poor Richard's Almanac*, had lots of commentaries on proper behavior. In the nineteenth century, hundreds of etiquette books were published, including the very popular *Youth's Educator for Home and Society*. This guidebook on manners and etiquette published in the late 19th century. Written by American author and journalist William B. Forbush, and aimed to educate young people on proper behavior in various social situations. The book covered topics such as table manners, dress, speech, and conduct in public places. It was widely distributed and used in schools and homes as a tool for teaching children and young adults how to behave in a polite and courteous manner in society.

Post World War II saw manners and etiquette undergo significant changes in society because of various factors such as the rise of feminism, the Civil Rights Movement, and the counterculture movement. These events led to a shift in societal norms and values, resulting in changes in acceptable behavior and attitudes. For example, the Civil Rights Movement led to the rejection of racial segregation and discrimination, while the rise of feminism challenged traditional gender roles and expectations. These changes influenced the development of new etiquette and manners that were more inclusive, diverse, and egalitarian.

Technology has brought significant changes to the way we communicate and interact with each other, which has influenced manners and etiquette in society. With the rise of social media and messaging platforms, there is now an expectation for people to respond quickly to messages and emails, leading to a blurring of boundaries between work and personal life. There is a new set of etiquette rules for online communication, such as avoiding all-caps messages, using proper spelling and grammar, and being mindful of tone and language when posting or commenting on social media. Using mobile phones has also changed the rules of etiquette, with many people using them during meetings, meals, and even in movie theaters. As a result, there is now a need for new rules and expectations for technology use in various social situations. More on that a little later in this book.

***

How Different Cultures Have Different Expectations For Manners and Etiquette

Different cultures have varying expectations for manners and etiquette. For example, in some cultures, they consider it polite to remove one's shoes when entering a home, while in others, they see it as a sign of disrespect. Similarly, the way people address one another, use utensils while eating, or even express emotions can differ across cultures. Understanding and respecting these cultural differences is important for effective communication and building positive relationships.

- In Japan, they consider it polite to bow instead of shaking hands when greeting someone.

- In many Middle Eastern countries, it is impolite to show the soles of your shoes, as they are seen as dirty.

- In some African countries, it is customary to eat with your hands instead of utensils.

- In China, burping after a meal is considered a compliment to the chef.

- In many Latin American countries, it is common to greet people with a kiss on the cheek, even if you are meeting them for the first time.

- In India, it is rude to eat with your left hand, as it is traditionally associated with bathroom duties.

- In South Korea, it is polite to pour drinks for others before filling your own glass.

- In Russia, it is customary to remove your shoes before entering someone's home.

- In Thailand, it is impolite to touch someone's head, as it is seen as the most sacred part of the body.

- In France, it is customary to greet people with a kiss on both cheeks, starting with the left.

- In Nigeria, it is disrespectful to eat or pass food with your left hand, as it is associated with bad luck.

- In some Native American cultures, it is impolite to make direct eye contact, as it is seen as a sign of aggression.

It is important for people to be aware of manners and etiquette in other countries because it shows respect for different cultures and can help avoid misunderstandings and unintended offense. Having knowledge of manners and etiquette can also help people navigate social situations and build positive relationships with people from different cultural backgrounds. Displaying proper manners and etiquette when traveling or interacting with individuals from other countries can reflect positively on one's own cultural background and may contribute to a more positive global community.

Have you traveled aboard? Did you come across any instances where there were differences between what you have learned and are accustomed to and to those you witnessed in your travels? Did your opinions change as you've gotten older or become a more seasoned traveler?

***

So, Why Do Manners and Etiquette Matter?

In today's world, manners and etiquette play an important role in establishing and maintaining positive relationships with others. They help to build trust, respect, and a sense of mutual understanding between people. By following basic rules of politeness and showing consideration for others, we can create an environment of civility and kindness, even amid disagreement or conflict. Manners and etiquette also show that we value and respect ourselves, as well as those around us. In a world where communication and relationships are increasingly digital and distant, practicing good manners and etiquette can help to foster a sense of human connection and empathy.

Understanding and practicing good manners and etiquette can make a tremendous difference in the way people feel about themselves and others. When individuals are mindful of their behavior and interactions, it can make those around them feel valued and respected.

Saying "please" and "thank you," giving compliments, showing up on time, and being attentive when others speak are all simple actions that can demonstrate consideration and respect. When people feel valued and respected, it can lead to stronger relationships, better communication, and a more positive and productive environment.

Practicing good manners and etiquette is important in building strong relationships with others. When we show respect and consideration towards others, we create a positive and welcoming environment that fosters trust and understanding. Good manners and etiquette can also help to avoid misunderstandings and conflicts, as clear communication and respectful behavior make it easier to connect with others and work towards common goals. By prioritizing manners and etiquette in our daily interactions, we can strengthen our relationships with family, friends, colleagues, and even strangers, ultimately leading to a more harmonious and fulfilling life.

Having good manners and following proper etiquette can have a positive impact on both your personal and professional life in countless ways. It helps you build a positive image and reputation, which can lead to more opportunities for career advancement and personal growth. In professional settings, practicing good manners and etiquette can help you build strong relationships with colleagues, clients, and customers, leading to better collaboration, improved communication, and increased trust. Similarly, in personal relationships, showing respect and consideration through good manners and etiquette can help foster strong and lasting connections with friends and family.

So let's remember, manners and etiquette have a rich history and have evolved over time, with different cultures having their own set of expectations. They are important as they promote positive human interactions, show respect and value for others, build relationships, and benefit both personal and professional lives. Understanding and practicing manners and etiquette can lead to success and a positive impact on society as a whole.

Answers to the quiz:

1. Etiquette

2. Etiquette

3. Manners

4. Etiquette

5. Etiquette

6. Manners

7. Etiquette

8. Etiquette

9. Manners

10. Etiquette

11. Manners

12. Etiquette

13. Etiquette

14. Etiquette

15. Manners

16. Etiquette

17. Manners

18. Manners

19. Etiquette

20. Manners

Chapter Four

The Art of Manners

"The world was my oyster but I used the wrong fork."—— Oscar Wilde

"E-mail has some magical ability to turn off the politeness gene in a human being."—— Jeff Bezos

"I was raised right — I talk about people behind their backs. It's called manners."—— Kathy Griffin

"Tweet others the way you want to be tweeted."
—— Germany Kent, You Are What You Tweet:
Harness the Power of Twitter to Create a Hap-
pier, Healthier Life

Making a Great First Impression

Making a great first impression is important because it sets the tone for many future interactions and can greatly affect how others perceive you. It can help build trust, establish credibility, and create positive relationships. A good first impression can open up opportunities in both personal and professional settings, while a negative one can close doors and limit potential growth. Therefore, it is essential to put your best foot forward and make a strong first impression.

Having a good foundation of manners and etiquette can help you make a great first impression in several ways:

- **It shows that you respect others:** Good manners involve being polite, courteous, and considerate towards others. By displaying these qualities, you convey to others that you respect them and value their presence.

- **It displays self-confidence:** When you know the rules of etiquette and follow them, you exude confidence and poise. This can be helpful when meeting new people or entering unfamiliar social situations.

- **It can help you navigate cultural differences:** Different cultures have different expectations for manners and etiquette. If you have a good understanding of these differences, you can avoid accidentally offending someone and instead show your respect for their culture.

- **It demonstrates your professionalism:** In a professional setting, good manners and etiquette are essential. By demonstrating that you understand these rules, you show you take your work seriously and are committed to presenting yourself in the best possible light.

We can't just talk about making good first impressions without bringing up the inevitable *bad* first impressions we all either have made or will make some day. Oh boy, we've all been there - that sinking feeling when you realize you've made a terrible first impression. Maybe you spilled your drink all over your new acquaintance, or accidentally insulted their pet poodle. But fear not, my friends! There are ways to recover from even the most cringe-worthy first meetings.

1. **Apologize:** If you said or did something offensive or inappropriate, apologize as soon as possible.

2. **Show interest:** Try to show interest in the other person's life or opinions and listen carefully to what they have to say.

3. **Be yourself:** Don't be someone you're not. Be genuine and let your personality shine through.

4. **Follow up:** If you get the person's contact information, follow up with a message or phone call to show that you're still interested in building a relationship.

5. **Make a good second impression:** Put extra effort into making a good second impression. Dress nicely, arrive on time, and be well-prepared.

6. **Use humor:** Humor can be a great way to break the ice and make people feel more comfortable around you.

7. **Offer a gesture of goodwill:** Offer to buy them a drink, send them a small gift, or do something nice to show that you're sincere.

8. **Ask for feedback:** Ask the other person for feedback on how you could improve your interaction or how you could have done better.

9. **Take responsibility:** If you made a mistake, take responsibility for it and try to make it right.

10. **Move on:** If all else fails, it's important to learn from the experience and move on. Don't dwell on the past, and focus on making positive first impressions in the future.

***

Common Courtesy

Common courtesy and basic manners are terms used interchangeably by many people. Common courtesy and basic manners refer to the common social behaviors that are expected of individuals in various settings. These behaviors include saying "please" and "thank you," holding doors for others, using polite language, and being respectful towards others. Basic manners are important as they help to establish positive interactions and build relationships with others. When individuals display basic manners, they show they value and respect the people around them. These behaviors are often taught in childhood, but they can be reinforced and improved throughout life. By maintaining good manners, individuals can make a positive impression and create a respectful and polite environment in all aspects of life.

As you will see throughout this book, society's notion of what we consider polite and respectful can quickly change and become obsolete. There are some pleasantries that have been around for decades, which are no longer being used.

Charlotte Hilton Andersen wrote an interesting article on Reader's Digest's website called, *16 Pleasantries People No Longer Say,* that illustrates this change. Below are a few of the examples she's compiled and her reasoning for people to no longer use them:

"I'm sorry"

"An apology was once considered a staple of polite society but it's falling out of favor—and not entirely for bad reasons, says Sharon Schweitzer, J.D., a modern manners expert, attorney, and founder of Access to Culture. In the past, it was used more of an expression of empathy but today it may be seen as a sign of weakness or confusion, she says. "Many coaches have recommended that women, especially, reduce the number of times that they start a sentence with 'I'm sorry, but...' and use more confident language instead," she explains."

"Missus" or "Miss"

"Similarly, addressing a woman as "Mrs." or"missus " is also increasingly seen as old-fashioned, and not in a cute way, Schweitzer says. Not only do these words presume gender, but they are also dependent on identifying the woman by her marital status, something she may not want. In addition, "Miss" can make a woman feel as if she's being seen as younger or talked down to. "Mrs. or Miss are not appropriate titles to use in professional settings in the United States," she says. "Ms. is the preferred title unless someone specifically tells you otherwise."

"Ma'am"

"Old movie buffs will recognize the iconic greeting for women, complete with a deferential head tilt. However, this gender-specific acknowledgment may be going the way of the old Westerns that made it so popular, Schweitzer says. "You may still hear it in some places in the South and in the military but in most other parts of the USA, 'ma'am' may not always be appreciated," she says. Why? One reason is it may make women feel as if they are being called old, a particular insult in a society that prizes youth or at least looking youthful."

***

So, What Should Good Manners Look Like?

People with good manners are typically easy to spot, as their behavior is respectful and courteous. Some signs of good manners may include:

- They use polite language and avoid offensive or derogatory language.

- They show consideration for others, such as holding doors open or offering to help.

- They listen attentively and do not interrupt others while they are speaking.

- They are punctual and show up on time for appointments or meetings.

- They express gratitude and appreciation, saying "please" and "thank you" when appropriate.

- They are respectful of personal space and do not invade others' personal boundaries.

- They show empathy and try to understand others' perspectives.

- They dress appropriately for the occasion and follow dress codes, if there are any.

- They are mindful of their behavior and strive to avoid offending others or causing discomfort.

- They are adaptable to different social settings and can adjust their behavior accordingly. Some examples include:

1. **At work:** Be punctual, respectful, and polite to your colleagues and superiors. Use professional language and maintain a positive attitude. Avoid gossip and negative talk. Offer to help your colleagues when needed.

2. **In romantic relationships:** Show appreciation, kindness, and consideration towards your partner. Use respectful and loving language. Practice active listening and avoid interrupting or talking over them. Show interest in their hobbies and opinions. Be willing to compromise and work through conflicts in a respectful manner.

3. **In public spaces:** Be aware of your surroundings and respectful of others. Use polite language and avoid being loud or disruptive. Hold doors for others and offer your seat to those who may need it.

Follow social norms and guidelines, such as wearing appropriate attire or using proper table manners in restaurants.

Overall, exhibiting good manners will be easy to see in any social setting that involves showing respect, consideration, and kindness towards others while maintaining a positive and professional demeanor.

***

Teaching Our Children Good Manners

Teaching manners to children is a crucial aspect of their social development. It involves instilling in them the proper ways to interact with others, be it in social or formal settings. When children learn good manners at a young age, they grow up to become respectful, considerate, and empathetic adults.

Getting it right is also important, as children learn by example, and so it is essential for parents and caregivers to model good behavior. Children should be taught to say please and thank you, use polite language, show respect for elders and authority figures, and be mindful of others' feelings. Teaching children how to use utensils properly, sit properly at the table, and properly hold doors for others can also go a long way in building social skills.

Good manners in children also help them build self-confidence and positive self-image, which leads to better communication skills and problem-solving abilities. When children have good manners, they are more likely to succeed academically, socially, and professionally.

In today's world, where social media and technology have made social interactions more impersonal, teaching manners to children is more important than ever. It helps to foster better relationships, both personally and professionally, and enables children to navigate social situations with ease and confidence. Ultimately, teaching good manners to children is an investment in their future and sets them up for success in all aspects of life.

Teaching manners to kids can be challenging for a variety of reasons. One reason is that kids often have shorter attention spans and may have difficulty remembering and consistently applying social etiquette rules. Additionally, parents and caregivers may have different beliefs and values about what constitutes good manners, leading to confusion or inconsistency in teaching. It can also be difficult to navigate cultural and societal differences in manners, especially in a diverse and globalized world. However, it is important to get it right because manners play a crucial role in shaping a child's social and emotional development, preparing them for success throughout their lives.

So, as a parent, what forms of manners and etiquette can you start teaching and reinforcing to your children to help them become the well-mannered child of your dreams? Start with these:

- **Teaching them to say, "Please" and "Thank you"**: Teaching by example. Parents can start teaching their young children to say "please" and "thank you" by leading by example and demonstrating the behavior themselves and using positive reinforcement. For example, they can say "please" and "thank you" when interacting with their children and make sure to praise and reward them when they use these phrases. Additionally, parents can use games, songs, and stories to help their children understand the importance of showing gratitude and using polite language in social interactions.

- **Teaching them to wait their turn**: Parents can teach their young children to always wait their turn by setting clear expectations and boundaries, and consistently reinforcing them. They can create opportunities for their children to practice taking turns, such as during playtime or while waiting in line, and praise them for their patience and good behavior. It's also important to teach them when it is ok to interrupt someone, for example, if there is an emergency.

- **Learning to ask permission first**: By encouraging their child to ask before taking or using something that doesn't belong to them, and explaining why it's important to respect other people's belongings and personal space. Following up with positive reinforcement, as well as having set rules in place, such as answering phones, opening the front door, etc.

- **Learning when and how to say, Excuse me"**: Not only is saying, "Excuse me" is important for showing respect and consideration for others, it also should be used for the many times your child will come up and talk to you or ask you something while you are speaking with someone else or doing something. An example could be" "Excuse me, mom, I need to go to the bathroom." or "Excuse me, but I am not feeling well."

- **Not commenting on someone else's appearance or actions:** Parents can teach their young children not to comment on someone's appearance or behavior by modeling positive language and behavior themselves. They can explain that it is important to focus on people's actions and character rather than their appearance, and that it is not polite to make comments that could hurt someone's feelings. Parents can also encourage their children to ask questions if they are curious, but to do so in a respectful and non-judgmental way.

- **How to express gratitude in different ways:** Parents can teach their young children by consistently reminding their children to say "thank you" when receiving something or help from others. Parents can also encourage their children to write thank-you notes or draw pictures to express their appreciation. Another way is by involving children in acts of kindness and charity to help them understand the value of giving and receiving gratitude.

- **Teaching children to not use bad language or call someone a bad name:** First, parents must always be mindful of what they say and do, as it's an easy way for children to pick up bad behaviors. Parents can explain to their children the importance of using kind and respectful language and the negative impact that negative language can have on others. Additionally, parents can praise their children when they use appropriate language and remind them of the importance of being kind and respectful to others. Additionally, **teasing** others should also not be tolerated, as everyone has different levels of sensitivity, and you wouldn't want to hurt another, even if you were only joking around.

- **Teaching children to make offers of help and to always expect nothing in return:** Parents can help their children understand the value of helping others and the satisfaction that comes with doing something kind for someone else. Parents can also teach their children that it is important to offer help without expecting anything in return and to do it out of kindness and a desire to make a positive difference in someone else's life.

The art of manners is much more than just a set of rules that we follow in social settings. They are the building blocks of how we interact with others and communicate our respect and consideration towards them. When we engage in polite and considerate behavior, we not only show that we value and respect others, but we also build stronger connections and positive relationships with them.

Teaching our children good manners is an essential part of raising them to be successful and well-rounded individuals. By instilling the importance of manners from an early age, we set our children up for success in all areas of life. Not only does it help them build strong relationships, but it also enables them to make great first impressions in both personal and professional situations.

The art of manners can be particularly useful in navigating the different social settings that we may encounter throughout our lives. For example, in the workplace, good manners can be the key to building positive relationships with colleagues, creating a good impression with superiors, and establishing a professional reputation. In romantic relationships, manners and etiquette can help to foster trust, intimacy, and mutual respect between partners.

In public spaces, good manners and etiquette can make all the difference in creating a positive and harmonious environment for everyone. From simple gestures like holding the door open for someone or saying "excuse me," to more complex behaviors like practicing patience and listening actively, good manners help to create a culture of kindness and consideration that benefits everyone.

As society continues to evolve and technology advances, the way we interact with each other is changing. With the rise of social media and digital communication, it's more important than ever to understand the role of manners and etiquette in the digital age. The next part of this book will delve into how our online behavior can impact our personal and professional lives, and provide guidance on how to navigate this new world with grace and consideration. From email etiquette to social media dos and don'ts, mastering digital manners is an essential skill for modern-day communication. Let's dive in and explore how we can adapt traditional manners to the digital realm.

Chapter Five

Manners In The Digital Age

Social media and digital communication have revolutionized the way we interact with one another, both in positive and negative ways. On one hand, these platforms have made it easier to connect with people from all over the world, share our thoughts and ideas, and stay informed on current events. However, these same platforms have also created new challenges and obstacles with communicating effectively and respectfully.

One of the biggest changes brought about by social media and digital communication is the speed at which information travels. With the click of a button, we can share our thoughts and opinions with a global audience, potentially reaching thousands or even millions of people. This can be incredibly empowering, but it also means that we need to be extra mindful of what we say and how we say it.

Another challenge posed by social media and digital communication is the lack of face-to-face interaction. When we communicate online, we miss out on important cues like body language, tone of voice, and facial expressions. This can lead to misunderstandings, hurt feelings, and even conflicts that might have been avoided in person.

Social media and digital communication have also made it easier for people to hide behind anonymity and say things they might not otherwise say in person. Cyberbullying, trolling, and harassment have become major issues on these platforms, causing emotional distress and harm to many people.

In the following sections of this book, we will explore how the principles of good manners and etiquette can be applied in the digital age to help us navigate these new challenges and communicate effectively and respectfully in all settings.

***

The Importance of Manners In Online Interactions

As our communication has shifted more towards digital platforms, the importance of manners in online interactions has become increasingly important. While the rules of engagement may seem less formal than in face-to-face interactions, the impact of our online behavior can be just as significant.

One reason manners are so crucial in online interactions is that they shape how we are perceived by others. Online, we have to rely on written words and visuals to convey our message, and this can make it easier for our intentions to be misinterpreted. By using good manners, such as using polite language and avoiding aggression, we can minimize the risk of being misunderstood and build positive relationships.

Another important aspect of manners in online interactions is the need to respect boundaries. Digital platforms allow us to communicate with people from all over the world, and it's easy to forget that people have different cultural norms, beliefs, and values. It's important to be mindful of these differences and to approach online interactions with sensitivity and empathy. This can include avoiding topics that may be sensitive or offensive to others, and being respectful of people's time and privacy.

The speed and convenience of digital communication can sometimes lead to a lack of consideration for others. For example, it's common to see people post messages or comments without taking the time to proofread or consider the impact of their words. This can cause typos, misunderstandings, and hurt feelings. By taking the time to use good manners, such as proofreading messages and being thoughtful about what we post, we can avoid these issues and build stronger relationships online.

Manners are just as important in online interactions as they are in face-to-face interactions. By using good manners and being respectful of others, we can build positive relationships and make the most of the digital tools that are available to us.

***

Using Technology To Promote Kindness and Acts of Class

Technology has the power to connect people from all over the world and has revolutionized the way we communicate. Social media platforms and other digital tools have made it easier to stay in touch with loved ones, make new friends, and collaborate on projects. But in the age of social media, it's all too easy for people to forget the importance of good manners and kindness in their online interactions.

However, technology can also promote kindness and class. For example, social media can spread positive messages, share uplifting stories, and encourage people to be kinder to one another. Digital tools like messaging apps and video conferencing platforms can help us stay connected with people we care about, even if we can't be with them in person.

Technology has also created new opportunities for acts of kindness and class. Crowdfunding platforms, for example, enable people to support causes they care about and help those in need. Online forums and support groups provide a safe space for people to share their experiences and offer support to others.

In short, while technology has certainly changed the way we interact with one another, it can also be a powerful tool for promoting kindness and class. By using technology in a positive and respectful way, we can build stronger relationships, help others, and create a better world for all.

***

Modern Manners: Navigating Social Media

Navigating social media can be challenging, especially with demonstrating good manners and etiquette. With the proliferation of social media platforms, it has become easier for people to interact with one another, but it has also become easier for people to engage in negative behaviors, such as cyberbullying, trolling, and online harassment. According to a 2019 UNICEF poll, 33% of adolescents in 30 countries were victims of cyberbullying. In 2018, the Pew Research Center reported that 59% of U.S. youth had experience with cyberbullying such as offensive name calling, rumor spreading, and receiving unwanted images. In this digital age, it is essential to understand how to behave online, just as it is important to understand how to behave in face-to-face interactions.

One of the most important aspects of demonstrating good manners and etiquette online is to show respect for others. This means refraining from engaging in negative behaviors, such as posting hurtful comments, sharing inappropriate content, or spreading false information. It also means acknowledging others' opinions and beliefs, even if they differ from our own, and engaging in constructive discussions rather than attacking or belittling others.

Another important aspect of online manners and etiquette is being mindful of our online presence. This means being aware of what we post online, how we present ourselves, and how our online activities reflect on our character and reputation. We should also know the impact our online activities may have on others and avoid actions that could be perceived as disrespectful or hurtful.

It is essential to be aware of the online community's norms and expectations, as they may vary from platform to platform and culture to culture. For example, what may be acceptable to one platform may not be on another, and what may be appropriate in one culture may not be in another. It is important to be aware of these differences and adapt our behaviors accordingly.

Social media has become a ubiquitous part of modern life, and with it comes the need for individuals to understand the dos and don'ts of online communication. In today's world, authenticity is highly valued, and it's essential to be yourself on social media. However, with professional interactions, it's crucial to maintain a level of professionalism and etiquette.

One Do's of social media is to be authentic and true to yourself. Social media is an excellent platform to share your thoughts, ideas, and experiences, and doing so in a genuine way can help build connections with others. It's also important to engage with others in a respectful and polite manner, even if you disagree with them.

On the other hand, some of the Don'ts of social media include over sharing personal information, engaging in cyberbullying, and being disrespectful to others. While social media can be a powerful tool for networking and building relationships, it's important to remember that anything you post online is permanent and can have far-reaching consequences.

For professional interactions, it's crucial to strike a balance between being authentic and being professional. This means avoiding controversial or divisive topics, refraining from using vulgar language, and maintaining a positive tone. It's also important to be mindful of the image you're presenting online, as potential employers, clients, or business partners may research you online.

Navigating social media requires a strong understanding of manners and etiquette. By being authentic, respectful, and professional, individuals can use social media to build positive connections and advance their personal and professional goals.

***

Modern Manners: Texting Etiquette

Texting etiquette refers to the set of rules and guidelines that govern how people communicate with one another via text messages. It is important to remember that text messaging is a form of communication that is both convenient and efficient, but also has the potential to be misinterpreted or misconstrued. As such, it is essential to be mindful of one's tone and language when texting, as well as to observe basic rules of manners and etiquette.

Some of the key principles of texting etiquette include:

- **Be clear and concise:** Text messages are not the place for lengthy diatribes or complex discussions. Keep your messages short and to the point.

- **Use proper grammar and spelling.** While texting may seem informal, it is still important to use proper grammar and spelling to avoid confusion or misunderstandings.

- **Respect people's time.** Avoid sending texts late at night or early in the morning unless it is urgent or necessary.

- **Avoid texting while driving.** You would think this would be a no-brainer, but distracted driving is a leading cause of accidents, so it is important to avoid texting while operating a vehicle.

- **Do not text while you are walking around in public.** Be cognizant of your surroundings and of other people.

- **Don't text in the middle of a conversation.** If you are in the middle of a face-to-face conversation, it is impolite to pull out your phone and start texting.

- **DON'T USE ALL CAPS!** (see what I did there?) Typing in all caps is considered shouting and can be interpreted as aggressive or confrontational.

- **Don't send multiple texts in a row.** Sending multiple texts in a row can come across as pushy or demanding.

- **Don't share private or sensitive information.** Texting is not a secure form of communication, so it is important to avoid sharing private or sensitive information via text.

- **Don't text when you are angry or upset.** It is easy to say things in the heat of the moment that you may later regret. Take a moment to calm down before responding to a text that has upset you.

- **Don't ignore texts.** If someone has taken the time to send you a text, it is important to respond in a timely manner, even if it is just to let them know you received their message and will respond later.

***

Email Etiquette: Crafting Effective and Polite Messages

In today's digital age, email has become an integral part of communication in both personal and professional settings. However, with the convenience and speed of email, it's easy to forget about the importance of email etiquette. Poor email communication can damage relationships and create misunderstandings, while good email etiquette can help you make a positive impression and build strong connections.

Whether you're emailing a coworker, a client, or a friend, there are certain guidelines you should follow to ensure that your communication is clear, effective, and respectful. Here are some essential email etiquette tips to keep in mind for all situations:

- **Use a clear and concise subject line**. The subject line should accurately reflect the content of your email and give the recipient an idea of what to expect.

- **Address the recipient appropriately**. In a professional setting, use the recipient's title and last name (e.g. "Dear Mr. Smith"). In a personal setting, you can use their first name or a more informal greeting.

- **Use a professional email address.** If you're sending an email in a professional context, make sure your email address is appropriate and reflects positively on you.

- **Keep your message brief and to the point.** Be respectful of the recipient's time and avoid including unnecessary information or rambling.

- **Use proper grammar and spelling.** Poor grammar and spelling can make you come across as careless or unprofessional.

- **Avoid using all caps or excessive punctuation.** This can be perceived as shouting or being overly aggressive.

- **Be mindful of your tone.** Tone can be difficult to convey in written communication, so be careful to avoid language that could be misinterpreted or offensive.

- **Use a professional signature**. Your email signature should include your name, title, and contact information.

- **Be careful with attachments.** Only include attachments that are relevant to the email and make sure they are properly formatted and labeled.

- **Proofread before sending.** Always double-check your email before hitting send to ensure that it's error-free and conveys the message you intended.

In addition to these general email etiquette tips, there are some specific guidelines to follow for different situations:

Email etiquette for professional settings:

1. **Use a proper greeting.** When beginning an email, use a proper greeting such as "Dear [recipient's name]" or "Hello [recipient's name]". Avoid using informal greetings, such as "Hey" or "Hiya". If you are unsure of the recipient's name, use a general greeting such as "To Whom It May Concern" or "Dear Sir/Madam".

2. **Use a descriptive subject line that accurately reflects the content of the email.** Your email's subject line should be clear and concise, indicating the purpose of the email. This helps the recipient to understand what your email is about and how to prioritize it. Avoid using vague or misleading subject lines that can lead to confusion.

3. **Use a professional tone and avoid using slang or informal language.** Avoid using overly casual language or slang. Use a polite and respectful tone, even if you are expressing dissatisfaction or disagreement.

4. **Avoid sending emails outside of normal business hours unless it's an emergency.** Avoiding sending emails outside of normal business hours is important because it shows respect for others' time and work-life balance. When emails are sent during non-business hours, it can create an expectation

of immediate response and cause unnecessary stress for the recipient. Additionally, it can be seen as a boundary violation and negatively impact work relationships. Therefore, unless it is truly urgent and cannot wait until the next business day, it is best to avoid sending emails outside of normal business hours.

5. **Use a proper closing.** When ending an email, use a proper closing such as "Sincerely" or "Best regards". Avoid using informal closings such as "Cheers" or "Later". Sign off with your name, title, and contact information.

6. **Don't use email to discuss sensitive or confidential information.** Email is not a secure form of communication, and therefore should not be used to discuss sensitive or confidential information. If you need to discuss sensitive information, use a more secure method such as in-person meetings or phone calls.

7. **Respond to emails in a timely manner.** Delayed responses can lead to frustration and can appear unprofessional. Try to respond within 24-48 hours, even if it is just to acknowledge receipt of the email.

8. **Avoid forwarding chain emails or spam.** Forwarding chain emails or spam can be annoying and frustrating for the recipients, as they often clutter up their inbox and may contain irrelevant or inaccurate information. It can also be seen as unprofessional and a waste of time, particularly in a work setting where time is valuable and should be spent on important tasks. Additionally, forwarding chain emails or

spam can increase the risk of viruses and malware, potentially putting both the sender and the recipients at risk. Therefore, it's important to exercise good judgment and discretion when it comes to forwarding emails, and only do so when the content is relevant and appropriate for the intended recipient.

Email etiquette for job applications:

- **Use a clear and concise subject line that includes the position you're applying for. As an example:**

Subject: Application for Marketing Manager Position - John Doe

By including the position you're applying for in the subject line, you immediately convey to the recipient the purpose of the email. This makes it easier for the hiring manager or recruiter to identify and prioritize your email amongst the hundreds of other emails they receive daily. Additionally, including your name in the subject line helps to ensure that your email doesn't get lost or overlooked in the hiring process.

- **Customize your email for each job application.** Customizing an email for each job application is important because it shows the employer that the applicant has put in the effort to tailor their application specifically to that job. This indicates that the applicant is genuinely interested in the position and has taken the time to research the company and the job requirements. It also allows the applicant to highlight their skills and experiences that are most relevant to the job, making it easier for the employer to see why they would be a good fit for the position. In addition, a customized email demonstrates attention to detail and professionalism, which can make a positive impression on the employer.

- **Use a professional email address.** The last thing you would want to do is apply for your dream job and use an inappropriate email address, such as: igethigh247365@email.com

- **Use a formal tone and avoid using slang or informal language.** Using a formal tone and avoiding slang conveys professionalism and respect for the hiring manager or recruiter. It shows that the applicant takes the opportunity seriously and is willing to put effort into presenting themselves in a professional manner. Using informal language or slang can come across as unprofessional and may lead the hiring manager to question the applicant's communication skills or suitability for the job.

- **Attach your resume and cover letter as separate documents in the appropriate format.** It's important for several reasons. First, it ensures that the documents can be easily accessed and viewed by the employer. Second, it shows that the applicant is detail-oriented and understands the importance of presenting a professional image. Third, it allows the employer to easily save and file the documents for future reference. Fourth, it reduces the risk of formatting errors that may occur when copying and pasting information into the body of an email. Overall, attaching the resume and cover letter in the appropriate format shows that the applicant is organized, professional, and respectful of the employer's time and needs.

By following these email etiquette guidelines, you can ensure that your communication is clear, effective, and respectful in all situations.

Whether you're communicating with coworkers, clients, friends, or family, good email etiquette can help you build strong relationships and avoid misunderstandings.

***

Modern Manners: Workplace Etiquette

Workplace etiquette refers to the unwritten rules and codes of conduct that define the behavior of employees in a professional setting. It encompasses everything from dress code to interpersonal communication and is crucial for creating a positive and productive work environment.

One of the key aspects of workplace etiquette is the dress code. While it may vary from workplace to workplace, employees should always strive to dress appropriately for the situation. This means avoiding overly casual attire, wearing clean and well-maintained clothing, and avoiding clothing that is too revealing or provocative.

Another important aspect of workplace etiquette is communication. Employees should always strive to communicate in a professional and respectful manner, whether it be in person, via email, or over the phone. This includes using appropriate language, avoiding gossip or negative talk, and being mindful of tone and body language.

Workplace etiquette involves respecting the personal space and boundaries of others. This includes avoiding behavior that could be considered harassment, such as unwanted physical contact or inappropriate comments. It also means respecting the privacy of others, both in terms of physical space and digital communications.

Good workplace etiquette also involves being punctual and reliable. Employees should always strive to arrive on time for meetings and appointments, and to meet deadlines and deliverables. This shows respect for others' time and helps to maintain a positive and productive work environment.

Here are a few more examples of workplace etiquette that should be followed:

- **Use appropriate language.** Using appropriate language in the workplace is crucial for maintaining professionalism. Avoid using slang or offensive language.

- **Avoid gossiping.** Gossiping is unprofessional and can create a toxic work environment. Avoid participating in or spreading gossip.

- **Keep your workspace tidy.** A tidy workspace shows respect for your coworkers and creates a more organized and productive work environment.

- **Use technology appropriately.** Using technology inappropriately, such as using your phone during meetings or sending personal emails from work, can be disrespectful and unprofessional.

- **Actively listen.** Active listening is an important aspect of workplace etiquette. Pay attention to what others are saying and show respect by not interrupting or multitasking during conversations.

- **Be mindful of cultural differences.** Be mindful of cultural differences in the workplace, including language, customs, and behaviors.

- **Be courteous and respectful.** Above all, workplace etiquette is about being courteous and respectful to others. Treat your coworkers with kindness and professionalism to create a positive work environment.

Overall, workplace etiquette is essential for creating a professional and respectful workplace environment. By adhering to the unwritten rules and codes of conduct that govern workplace behavior, employees can foster positive relationships with colleagues and superiors, build their professional reputation, and contribute to a productive and successful workplace culture.

***

Handling Conflicts at Work With A Coworker or Boss

Conflict is a natural part of working in any organization, and it can arise from differences in opinions, values, or personalities. However, it's crucial to learn how to handle conflicts professionally to maintain a positive and healthy work environment. Here are some of the best ways to handle conflicts at work with coworkers or bosses:

- **Stay calm.** When you're in a heated argument or conflict, it's essential to keep your emotions in check. Take a deep breath, step back, and try to approach the situation calmly and rationally.

- **Listen actively.** Listen carefully to the other person's perspective, and try to understand their point of view. Make sure you ask clarifying questions to ensure that you fully understand their position.

- **Express your concerns.** Clearly express your own concerns, but avoid blaming or attacking the other person. Stick to the facts and avoid exaggerating or making assumptions.

- **Find common ground.** Look for areas of agreement and try to find a compromise that both parties can accept. Be open to different ideas and perspectives, and be willing to make concessions.

- **Collaborate.** Work together to find a solution that benefits everyone involved. Be open to different approaches and be willing to try new things.

- **Seek mediation.** If you're unable to resolve the conflict on your own, consider seeking help from a neutral third party, such as a mediator. A mediator can help facilitate a conversation and find common ground.

- **Escalate the issue.** If the conflict is severe or you're unable to resolve it on your own, consider escalating the issue to your supervisor or HR representative. Be prepared to provide evidence of the conflict and specific examples of the behavior that's causing the conflict.

- **Follow up.** After you've resolved the conflict, follow up with the other person to ensure that the issue is truly resolved. Be willing to make changes and be open to feedback.

- **Learn from the experience.** Conflict can be an opportunity to learn and grow. Reflect on the experience and consider what you could have done differently. Use the experience to develop your conflict resolution skills and become a better communicator.

Unfortunately, conflicts are inevitable in any workplace, but they don't have to be destructive. By staying calm, listening actively, expressing your concerns, finding common ground, collaborating, seeking mediation, escalating the issue if necessary, following up, and learning from the experience, you can resolve conflicts in a positive and productive way. Remember that conflict resolution is a skill that takes practice, so be patient and persistent in your efforts to become a better communicator and problem solver.

***

Dating In The Workplace

Dating in the workplace can be a tricky situation to navigate, particularly when it comes to dating coworkers or bosses. While some companies have policies against workplace relationships altogether, others may allow them under certain circumstances. But regardless of whether your company has a policy or not, there are both good and bad reasons to consider before pursuing a relationship with a coworker or boss.

Statistics show that workplace relationships are fairly common, with a survey by **CareerBuilder** finding that 41% of workers have dated a coworker. Of those, 30% have gone on to marry their coworker. However, while some workplace relationships can lead to long-term, happy relationships, many others end in heartbreak and awkwardness.

If you do decide to pursue a relationship with a coworker or boss, it's important to set clear boundaries and be prepared for the potential consequences. If things don't work out, you'll still have to see each other at work, which can be uncomfortable and distracting. Additionally, if the relationship becomes public knowledge, it can create tension and gossip in the workplace.

One good reason to consider dating a coworker or boss is that you already have a shared interest and may have a lot in common due to working together. Additionally, dating someone you work with can make it easier to understand each other's schedules and the demands of the job. It can also be a way to form a deeper connection with someone you already know and trust.

However, there are also many bad reasons to consider dating a coworker or boss. For example, if you're using the relationship as a way to advance your career or gain special treatment, that's a red flag. Similarly, if you're only pursuing the relationship because you're bored or lonely, that's not a healthy basis for a relationship and can lead to a messy breakup.

Another consideration when it comes to dating in the workplace is when to involve HR. If your company has a policy against workplace relationships, it's important to inform HR before you begin dating to avoid potential conflicts of interest. Additionally, if you feel uncomfortable or harassed by a coworker or boss who is pursuing a relationship with you, it's important to report it to HR as soon as possible.

All of that being said, dating in the workplace can be a complex and potentially risky situation. It's important to weigh the pros and cons and consider both good and bad reasons before pursuing a relationship with a coworker or boss. If you do decide to proceed, it's crucial to communicate openly and honestly, set clear boundaries, and be prepared for the potential consequences. And if things do go wrong, it's important to handle the situation with maturity and professionalism to avoid causing disruption in the workplace.

Chapter Six

Socializing Like a Pro: Parties, Weddings, and Other Events

Socializing like a pro is a skill that goes beyond simply knowing which fork to use or how to shake hands. It encompasses a range of social behaviors that are essential for building relationships, navigating social situations, and ultimately succeeding in life.

For young people who have grown up in the digital age, socializing in person may not come as naturally as it did for previous generations. Social media and technology have given rise to a generation of digital natives who are accustomed to communicating through screens rather than face-to-face. As a result, they may lack the confidence and skills necessary to navigate social situations with ease.

This is where manners and etiquette come in. While they may seem old-fashioned or outdated to some, they are still incredibly relevant in today's world. Good manners and etiquette help to create a positive and respectful atmosphere, make others feel at ease, and ultimately foster stronger relationships.

When it comes to socializing like a pro, it's important to first understand the fundamental principles of good manners and etiquette. This includes things like showing respect, being courteous, and showing consideration for others. These principles apply in all social situations, from the workplace to personal relationships to social gatherings.

One key aspect of socializing like a pro, is the ability to communicate effectively. This means not only being able to express yourself clearly and confidently, but also being an active listener. Good communication involves being present and engaged, asking questions, and demonstrating empathy and understanding.

Another important aspect of socializing like a pro, is knowing how to navigate social settings with ease. This includes things like knowing how to introduce yourself, how to start and maintain a conversation, and how to gracefully exit a conversation when it's time to move on. It also involves being aware of social cues and being able to read the room in order to adjust your behavior accordingly.

Besides these fundamental principles, there are several specific manners and etiquette practices that can be useful in social situations. For example, being mindful of personal space and physical boundaries is important for making others feel comfortable and respected. It's also important to be aware of cultural differences and to show respect for different customs and traditions.

Socializing like a pro also involves being aware of your own behavior and how it may be perceived by others. This includes things like your body language, tone of voice, and overall demeanor. Being mindful of these things can help to project confidence and competence, and can ultimately lead to more positive social interactions.

For young people who may not have had as much experience in social situations, it's important to build these skills early on. We can do this through a variety of means, such as reading books like this one, taking etiquette classes or taking part in social clubs or organizations. It's also important for parents and educators to model good manners and etiquette, and to encourage young people to practice these behaviors in their daily lives.

Ultimately, socializing like a pro is about building strong, respectful relationships with others. It requires a combination of fundamental principles, specific manners and etiquette practices, and an overall awareness of how your behavior impacts others. By cultivating these skills early on, young people can set themselves up for success in all aspects of their lives, from personal relationships to career success.

In this chapter, we will explore the nuances of manners and etiquette in various social events, including parties, weddings, and other special occasions. We will delve into the customs and expectations that come with attending these events, as well as provide guidance on how to conduct oneself with poise and grace. Whether it's navigating a crowded cocktail party, being a gracious wedding guest, or simply mingling with new acquaintances, having a solid understanding of proper manners and etiquette can make all the difference in creating a positive and memorable social experience. So, let's dive in and learn how to navigate these social events with confidence and ease.

***

Informal Etiquette: Parties, Gatherings, Public Places, etc.

So, you've been invited to a party or a mixer. Maybe some work friends invited you to join them out for after-work drinks or to get a bite to eat. You want to make a good impression, and even though these may be just your work colleagues, or even scarier, mostly complete strangers at a party, you are going to be judged by how you carry yourself, what you say, and what you do. For introverts and those of us whose social skills are poor or non-existent, here are some helpful manners and etiquette to follow to help you be invited back.

Let's start with work-related events or gatherings. Work-related social gatherings are a unique blend of social and professional elements. They offer a chance to get to know colleagues better, make new connections outside your department or company, and leave a lasting impression. Additionally, they provide an opportunity to network and interact with your supervisor in a more relaxed setting than a typical workday.

Listed below are some helpful suggestions for work-related gatherings:

- Introducing yourself to new colleagues or clients with a firm handshake and a smile, and remembering their name when you see them again.

- Engaging in small talk that is appropriate for the setting, such as asking about their work or interests, and avoiding controversial topics.

- Offering to get drinks or appetizers for others, or at least making sure that everyone has what they need.

- Being polite and courteous to everyone, including wait staff or other service personnel.

- Avoiding excessive alcohol consumption or inappropriate behavior, which could reflect poorly on your professionalism.

- Following the dress code or suggested attire for the event, to show that you understand the expectations and are willing to comply.

- Avoiding monopolizing conversations or interrupting others, and instead actively listening to what they have to say.

- Offering to connect with colleagues or clients on social media or through email, to continue building professional relationships.

- Refraining from using your phone during the event, or at least stepping away from the group if you need to take a call or respond to a message.

- Thanking the host or organizers of the event and expressing appreciation for the opportunity to attend.

- Avoiding making negative comments or complaining about work-related issues, which could make others uncomfortable or create a negative impression.

- Respecting cultural differences or preferences in food, music, or other aspects of the event.

- Following the lead of more senior colleagues or executives in terms of behavior and conversations, to avoid any missteps or misunderstandings.

- Showing interest in the work or projects of others and offering your own insights or suggestions if appropriate.

- Following up with colleagues or clients after the event, to continue building professional relationships and following up on any potential opportunities or leads.

In social situations, having good manners and etiquette is crucial for success and incredibly important for building strong relationships, both personally and professionally. These skills help to create a positive and respectful environment, which fosters better communication and understanding among individuals.

When it comes to any type of social gatherings, having good manners and etiquette is essential for making a positive first impression. It shows others that you are respectful, considerate, and interested in their well-being. This can lead to a more enjoyable experience for everyone involved, as people are more likely to open up and engage with others who demonstrate these qualities.

Additionally, having good manners and etiquette can help to avoid misunderstandings and conflicts. For example, using appropriate language and tone can prevent unintentional offense or miscommunication. Being mindful of others' personal space and boundaries can also help to avoid conflict and discomfort in social situations.

On the other hand, poor manners and etiquette can have negative consequences both in the short and long term. In the short term, it can lead to uncomfortable and awkward situations for both yourself and others. This can lead to a negative perception of you by others, making it difficult to form new relationships or maintain existing ones.

Long term, poor manners and etiquette can have even more significant consequences. It can damage your reputation, both personally and professionally, and limit your opportunities for growth and success. For example, if you are constantly rude or disrespectful to others, it may become difficult to find people who are willing to work with or recommend you.

Moreover, having poor manners and etiquette can also limit your personal growth and development. It can make it difficult to build and maintain healthy relationships, which are essential for personal and professional success. It can also prevent you from learning and growing from your experiences, as you may be less likely to receive constructive feedback or take responsibility for your actions.

By following these guidelines below, you can ensure that you are making the most out of your social interactions and leaving a lasting positive impression on those around you:

- **Introducing yourself and others.** Properly introducing yourself and others can help make everyone feel comfortable and included in a social gathering.

- **Using polite language.** Using polite language and avoiding profanity or offensive language can show respect and consideration for others.

- **Holding the door.** Holding the door for others, especially those who may need help, can reveal kindness and thoughtfulness.

- **Offering to help.** Offering to help someone who may struggle with something, such as carrying a heavy load, can show kindness and consideration.

- **Saying "please" and "thank you".** Using polite expressions such as "please" and "thank you" can signal gratitude and respect.

- **Respecting personal space.** Respecting personal space and avoiding getting too close to others can show consideration for their comfort level.

- **Being punctual.** Being on time for a social gathering can show respect for the host and other guests who are waiting.

- **Dressing appropriately.** Dressing appropriately for the occasion can show respect for the host and displays a willingness to participate in the event.

- **Offering compliments.** Offering sincere compliments to others can help make them feel valued and appreciated.

- **Being a good listener.** Being an attentive listener can show an interest in others and help build meaningful connections.

- **Avoiding gossip.** Avoiding gossip and negative talk can show maturity and respect for others' privacy and feelings.

- **Sharing food and drinks.** Offering to share food and drinks with others can show generosity and create a sense of community.

- **Keeping your phone away.** Keeping your phone away and being present in the moment shows respect for others and the event.

- **Cleaning up after yourself.** Cleaning up after yourself, whether it's at a party or in a public space, can show consideration for others and help maintain a clean environment.

- **Saying goodbye.** Saying goodbye to the host and other

guests before leaving can show gratitude and respect for the event and the people involved.

***

Formal Etiquette: Weddings, Dinners, Networking Events, etc.

Ah, formal events - a time to dust off the fancy dress, polish your shoes, and brush up on your etiquette! Whether you're attending a wedding, dinner party, or networking event, it's essential to know the do's and don'ts of formal etiquette. While the rules may seem stuffy or outdated, they can actually help you navigate these social situations with ease and grace. In this section, we'll explore the world of formal etiquette and help you navigate your way through, so you'll worry less about using the right fork, and more about enjoying the event. So check yourself in the mirror one last time, take a deep breath, and smile, because you got this!

Formal etiquette is a set of social customs that govern behavior in formal settings, such as weddings, dinners, and networking events. These settings have specific rules of conduct that are designed to make everyone feel comfortable and ensure that the event runs smoothly. Over the years, formal etiquette has evolved and changed to keep pace with changes in society, but the basic principles remain the same.

One of the main differences between formal and informal or casual etiquette is the level of formality expected. Formal events typically require a higher level of etiquitte, with guests expected to dress appropriately and behave in a manner that is respectful and dignified. In contrast, casual events allow for a more relaxed atmosphere and more casual dress and behavior.

At formal events like weddings, there are several customs and expectations that guests are expected to follow. For example, guests are expected to RSVP to the invitation in a timely manner, arrive on time, and dress appropriately for the occasion. The dress code for a formal wedding may include black tie or white tie, and guests are expected to dress accordingly. Women may wear long dresses or formal pantsuits, while men may wear tuxedos or dark suits.

During the ceremony, guests should remain quiet and respectful, refraining from talking or using their phones. It is important to follow the lead of the officiant and not make any sudden movements or noises that may disrupt the ceremony. After the ceremony, guests should greet the newlyweds and congratulate them. This is also a good time to take any photos or selfies, but it is important to be mindful of others and not take up too much time or space.

At formal dinners, guests are expected to follow a specific order of service and use proper table manners. This includes using the correct utensils for each course, placing the napkin on their lap, and waiting for everyone to be served before beginning to eat. It is also important to be mindful of the conversation and avoid topics that may be controversial or offensive. Guests should also be mindful of their alcohol consumption and not overindulge, as this can lead to inappropriate behavior.

Networking events are another example of a formal setting where etiquette is important. These events are typically designed to allow professionals to meet and make connections, and it is important to approach them with a professional demeanor. Guests should dress appropriately for the occasion and be prepared to introduce themselves and talk about their profession or interests. It is important to be respectful of others' time and not monopolize conversations or interrupt others. Guests should also exchange business cards if appropriate and follow up with any contacts they make after the event.

The importance of knowing the difference between formal and informal or casual etiquette cannot be overstated. Knowing how to behave in a formal setting can help you make a good impression and create positive relationships with others. In contrast, behaving inappropriately can lead to negative consequences such as damaged relationships, lost opportunities, and even legal trouble in extreme cases.

Formal etiquette is an important aspect of social interaction in settings, such as weddings, dinners, and networking events. Understanding the customs and expectations of these settings and following proper etiquette can help you make a good impression and create positive relationships with others. Behaving inappropriately can have serious consequences and should be avoided at all costs. By paying attention to the details and following proper etiquette, you can navigate formal settings with ease and confidence.

Here are some basic, but important, guides to follow:

- **Dress appropriately.** Dressing appropriately for the occasion is important when attending any formal event. Dress in formal attire that matches the dress code. This shows respect for the event and the host.

- **Be punctual.** Arriving on time or even a few minutes early to formal events is considered good etiquette. Being punctual shows that you respect the event and the host.

- **RSVP.** If an invitation requires an RSVP, respond in a timely manner. This allows the host to plan accordingly.

- **Greet others properly.** When attending formal events,

greet others with a proper handshake and a smile. It's also important to use their name, preferred pronouns, and make eye contact.

- **Table manners.** Proper table manners are crucial during formal dinners. Use the correct utensils and eat quietly and slowly. Also, wait until everyone at the table is served before eating.

- **Be mindful of alcohol consumption.** When attending formal events, it's important to drink responsibly. Overindulging in alcohol can lead to inappropriate behavior.

- **Offer to help.** If you are a guest at a formal event, offer to help the host with any tasks they may need assistance with.

- **Use appropriate language:.** Using appropriate language and refraining from using profanity or inappropriate language is essential when attending formal events.

- **Respect cultural differences**. When attending formal events that may involve different cultures, it's important to be respectful and mindful of cultural differences.

- **Don't overstay your welcome.** When attending formal events, it's important to be mindful of the end time and not overstay your welcome.

- **Be present.** When attending formal events, put away your phone and be present in the moment. This shows respect for the event and the people attending.

- **Bring a gift.** When attending formal events, it's customary to bring a gift for the host. This shows appreciation and gratitude for the invitation. *(Many bring a bottle of wine. Later in the book, I go into why this is **not** a good idea.)*

- **Network appropriately.** When attending networking events, be professional and approachable. Make sure to exchange business cards and follow up with any connections made.

- **Thank the host.** After attending a formal event, it's important to thank the host for their hospitality and for inviting you to the event. A thank-you note or email is always appreciated.

***

The Art of Conversation: Making Small Talk, Avoiding Awkward Silences, and More

Welcome to the section on the Art of Conversation! Whether you're at a networking event, a dinner party, or even just in a casual setting, being able to engage in meaningful conversations is a valuable skill that can help you make connections, build relationships, and even advance in your career. However, for some, making small talk can be a daunting task, and awkward silences can be uncomfortable. But fear not! In this section, we will explore the tips and tricks to help you become a master of conversation, from starting and maintaining engaging small talk to avoiding those dreaded awkward silences. So, let's dive in and learn how to confidently navigate any social situation with ease and charm!

What is small talk? Some would say that small talk is chit chatting or schmoozing or just shooting the breeze. Small talk is a light conversation that people engage in to break the ice and establish a connection with someone they don't know very well. It typically involves topics that are not too personal or controversial, such as the weather, sports, movies, or current events. Small talk can happen in various social situations, such as at parties, networking events, or in the workplace. The purpose of small talk is to establish a rapport with the other person and create a more relaxed and comfortable atmosphere for further conversation.

For some people, socializing and making small talk can be a real challenge. This is especially true for introverts, who tend to feel drained by social interactions and may struggle to come up with things to say in group settings. Additionally, people who have primarily interacted with others through technology may find it difficult to make conversation in person. They may be used to communicating through text messages or social media, which don't require the same level of social skills as face-to-face interactions. However, while these challenges can make socializing feel daunting, there are techniques and strategies that can help people feel more comfortable and confident in social situations. By learning the art of conversation and practicing these skills, even the most introverted or technologically dependent individuals can improve their social abilities and feel more at ease in social settings.

So, for those looking for some helpful hints, as well as, for those who would rather be stabbed in the eye then to be at a social event where they would have to interact with someone, here are some survival tips:

- **Prepare conversation starters.** One of the reasons people may feel anxious in social situations is not knowing what to say. Preparing a few conversation starters or topics ahead of time can help to ease this anxiety and give them a sense of control over the conversation. Some good topics to use are: hobbies or interests, travel, food or restaurants, sports, and pop culture. Best to avoid: politics, religion, personal finances, gossip, intimate relationships, controversial or sensitive social issues. Here are a few examples of conversation starters:

"What brought you to this event?"

"How do you know the host/hostess for this party?"

"Have you tried any of the food or drinks yet? What's your favorite so far?"

"What's the most interesting thing you've done recently?"

"What kind of music do you like? Have you been to any good concerts lately?"

"Have you traveled anywhere recently? Where's your favorite place you've been?"

"What do you think of the event so far?"

"Do you enjoy reading? What's your favorite book?"

"Hey, I love your [accessory or clothing item]. Where did you get it?"

"What do you like to do for fun?"

- **Practice active listening.** Rather than worrying about what to say next, focus on being present in the moment and actively listening to the other person. Ask open-ended questions and follow-up questions to show that you are interested and engaged.

- **Rising to greet someone.** Be sure to keep your arms by your side rather than in your pockets or on your hips. Don't forget to make eye contact. Standing up is a way to show respect, while remaining seated can be seen as a sign of disrespect towards the other person.

- **Find common ground.** Look for shared interests or experiences that you can discuss with the other person.

- **Use body language.** Body language and eye contact are crucial aspects of communication and play a significant role in manners. They can convey confidence, interest, respect, and sincerity. Proper body language and eye contact show that you are engaged in the conversation and attentive to the other person. In contrast, poor body language and lack of eye contact can send negative signals, such as disinterest or disrespect. Paying attention to your body language and maintaining good eye contact are essential components of good manners.

- **Smiling.** Smiling is a simple yet powerful gesture that can make a big difference in social interactions. Not only does it convey warmth and positivity, but it also signals to others that you are approachable and open to communication. By smiling more often, you can make yourself and those around you feel more at ease, leading to more pleasant and successful interactions.

- **Handshaking.** Handshaking is an essential part of social etiquette and can speak volumes about a person's confidence and demeanor. The strength of the handshake is essential, as it should be firm but not too tight. A limp handshake can indicate a lack of confidence, while an overly aggressive handshake can be uncomfortable and even painful for the other person.

The length of time shaking hands should be brief, lasting only a few seconds. Lingering for too long can make the other person feel awkward and uncomfortable. Additionally, maintaining eye contact during the handshake shows respect and indicates sincerity.

When it comes to shaking hands with women, it is essential to remember that women are equals and should be treated as such. A man should shake a woman's hand just as he would any other person's hand, with a firm grip and appropriate eye contact. It is essential to avoid any patronizing behavior, such as patting a woman's hand or treating her differently than a man.

- **Use humor.** A well-timed joke or lighthearted comment can help break the ice and make the other person feel more comfortable.

- **Avoid controversial topics.** Unless you know the other person well and are sure of their opinions, avoid discussing controversial topics such as politics or religion.

- **Share your own experiences.** Share your own stories or experiences related to the topic of conversation to keep it flowing.

- **Keep it light.** Avoid delving into deep or heavy topics and instead keep the conversation light and enjoyable.

- **Pay attention to the other person's cues.** If the other person seems uncomfortable or disinterested, shift the conversation to a new topic or wrap it up gracefully.

- **Be present in the moment.** Avoid checking your phone or letting your mind wander during the conversation. Stay focused on the person in front of you.

- **Join a group or class.** Joining a group or taking a class in an area of interest can be a great way to meet like-minded people and practice social skills in a structured setting.

- **Take deep breaths**. Deep breathing can help to calm nerves and reduce anxiety. Encourage the person to take a few deep breaths before entering a social situation, and to continue deep breathing if they feel overwhelmed.

- **Seek professional help.** If shyness and social anxiety are interfering with someone's daily life, it may be helpful to seek the assistance of a mental health professional. Cognitive-behavioral therapy (CBT) can be particularly effective in helping people overcome social anxiety and improve social skills.

- **Practice.** Like any skill, the art of conversation takes practice. Take every opportunity to practice making small talk and engaging in conversations with new people.

***

How To Be A Great Guest: What To Bring, How To Behave, and More

Being invited to someone's home or event is an honor and a privilege. As a guest, it is important to make a good impression and show appreciation for the host's hospitality. However, being a great guest goes beyond just showing up on time and bringing a gift. It's about respecting the host's home and rules, making an effort to engage with other guests, and being gracious and considerate throughout the event.

In this section, we will explore how to be a great guest, including what to bring, how to behave, and more. Whether you're attending a dinner party, game night, or any other social event, these tips will help you become a sought-after guest and ensure that you're always invited back.

- Bring a thoughtful and an appropriate gift, such as a bouquet of flowers, or a small housewarming present.

- Offer to help with preparations or clean up after the meal.

- Dress appropriately for the occasion, taking cues from the host or hostess.

- Arrive on time or just a few minutes late, but never too early.

- Be respectful of the host's home and belongings, including following any house rules or requests.

- Engage in polite conversation, showing interest in the host's life and experiences.

- Be mindful of other guests and try to make everyone feel welcome and included.

- Offer to bring a dish or contribute to the meal if requested or appropriate.

- Follow any dietary restrictions or preferences provided by the host.

- Offer to help serve or clean up after the meal.

- Thank the host for their hospitality and express gratitude for the invitation.

- Follow up with a thank-you note or message after the event.

***

Table Manners: How To Dine With Grace and Confidence

When it comes to dining, having proper table manners is crucial in showing respect to your host, as well as displaying confidence and sophistication in social settings. Whether it's a fancy dinner party, a business lunch, or a family gathering, knowing how to navigate a table with grace and poise can make all the difference in making a positive impression. From setting the table to using utensils, to knowing how to handle tricky foods, there are a variety of aspects to consider when it comes to dining etiquette. In this section, we will cover everything you need to know to dine with confidence and grace, so you can focus on enjoying your meal and the company around you. So, pull up a chair, and let's get started on this delicious journey of table manners and dining with grace and confidence!

When dining in a formal setting, you may be presented with an array of utensils, each with a specific purpose. It's important to know how to use each one properly to avoid any potential embarrassment. The basic rule of thumb is to start with the utensils on the outside and work your way in with each course. The first set of utensils will probably be the salad fork and the soup spoon. The salad fork will be smaller and the soup spoon larger. The next set will include the dinner fork and the dinner knife. The dinner fork will have four tines and the knife will have a serrated edge. After that, you may encounter a fish fork and knife, a dessert fork and spoon, and a bread knife. It's important to note that the bread knife should only be used for bread and not for cutting any other food.

Knowing how to hold your utensils properly when dining is an essential part of good table manners. It not only shows respect for the food, but also for the people around you. The basic rule is to hold the fork in the left hand and the knife in the right hand. The fork is used to pick up food, while the knife is used to cut it. However, the exact way to hold your utensils can vary depending on the type of food you are eating and the culture you are in. Learning these nuances can help you feel more confident and comfortable when dining in different settings.

Now that you are ready to show the world your newfound knowledge with using the correct utensil, it's time to show the other etiquette skills you have mastered, such as:

- **Take cues from others.** If you are unsure how to eat a particular dish, observe what others are doing and follow suit.

- **Ask for guidance.** If you are really struggling, discreetly ask a knowledgeable guest or the server for guidance.

- **Use utensils properly.** Make sure you are using the correct utensils for each dish, and hold them properly to avoid fumbling or making a mess.

- **Practice at home.** If you know you will be encountering a particular dish, try practicing at home so you feel more confident when dining out.

- **Cut food into small pieces.** If you are unsure how to eat something large or awkwardly shaped, cut it into smaller, more manageable pieces.

- **Use a napkin**. If a dish is particularly messy, use your napkin to dab your mouth or hands discreetly.

- **Don't make a big deal out of it.** If you do make a mistake or spill something, don't draw attention to it or make a big deal out of it. Simply apologize if necessary and move on.

- **Take your time.** Don't rush through a meal or a particular dish. Take your time and savor each bite.

- **Be open-minded.** Remember that fine dining often involves trying new and unique dishes. Approach each new dish with an open mind and a willingness to try something new.

- **Enjoy the experience.** Fine dining is meant to be a luxurious and enjoyable experience. Don't get too caught up in worrying about tricky foods or perfect table manners, and instead focus on enjoying the company and the delicious cuisine.

***

The Art of Hosting: Planning, Preparing, and Executing a Successful Event

Good manners and etiquette are essential elements of successful event hosting. Proper behavior and social graces can make guests feel welcomed, comfortable, and appreciated. The art of hosting also involves creating an atmosphere of warmth and hospitality, anticipating guests' needs, and making them feel special. A good host must also manage the flow of the event, making sure guests are entertained and the evening runs smoothly. Overall, good manners and etiquette are the foundation of successful event hosting, ensuring that guests feel valued and appreciated.

Hosting a dinner party, cocktail soirée, or any other type of social gathering in your home can be a thrilling and rewarding experience. Being able to welcome guests into your own space, showcase your culinary skills, and create an atmosphere that encourages lively conversation and laughter is a great feeling. Hosting an event can be both exhilarating and overwhelming, especially if you're not accustomed to the planning and execution of a successful event. From the menu to the guest list to the decorations, every aspect requires careful thought and attention to detail. But don't worry, with a little bit of planning and preparation, you can host an event that will be the talk of the town (in a good way!).

First and foremost, it's important to determine the purpose of the event. Is it a casual get-together or a formal dinner party? Is it a celebration of a milestone or simply an excuse to have some fun? Once you have a clear idea of the purpose, you can start planning the guest list and the invitations.

When planning the guest list, be sure to consider the size of your venue and the type of event you're hosting. For example, if you're hosting a formal dinner party, you'll want to limit the guest list to close friends and family. On the other hand, if you're hosting a more casual get-together, you can invite a larger group of people.

Once you have your guest list, it's time to send out the invitations. You can either send traditional paper invitations or opt for a more modern approach, such as an e-vite or social media event page. Just be sure to include all of the important details, such as the date, time, location, and dress code (if applicable).

Next, it's time to plan the menu. This can be one of the most challenging aspects of hosting an event, as you want to ensure that everyone's dietary needs and preferences are met. If you're not confident in your cooking abilities, consider hiring a caterer or purchasing pre-made food items.

When planning the menu, be sure to consider the theme of the event and the time of day. For a casual daytime event, you might opt for finger foods and light snacks. For a formal dinner party, you'll want to serve a multi-course meal with a variety of options for appetizers, entrees, and desserts.

The table setting for a fine dining experience at home can be quite elaborate and formal. As the host, start by laying a crisp, clean tablecloth over the table, and then set the table with fine china, crystal glassware, and polished silverware. The place setting should be arranged symmetrically, with the dinner plate in the center, the fork on the left, the knife on the right, and the spoon to the right of the knife. The bread plate and butter knife should be placed above the forks, and the water glass should be placed above the knife. Finally, the napkin can be placed on top of the dinner plate, folded or rolled in a decorative manner. Once the table is set, you can add finishing touches such as flowers, candles, or other decorations to create a beautiful and elegant atmosphere for the guests.

In addition to the menu and décor, it's important to consider the entertainment. This can include everything from music to games to a photo booth. Be sure to choose entertainment that is appropriate for the type of event you're hosting and the preferences of your guests.

As the host, it's important to be prepared for anything that might arise during the event. This includes having a first aid kit on hand, having extra food and drinks available, and being ready to handle any unexpected situations with grace and humor.

When it comes to executing a successful event, the key is to stay organized and focused. Make a checklist of everything you need to do before the event, and be sure to check off each item as it's completed. On the day of the event, be sure to delegate tasks to trusted friends or family members, so that you can focus on being a gracious host.

Remember, hosting an event is all about creating a memorable experience for your guests. By planning and preparing ahead of time, you can ensure that your event is a success and that your guests have a great time. And who knows, you might just discover that you have a knack for event planning and become the go-to host among your friends and family. Next Thanksgiving dinner is now at your house!!

***

The Do's and Don'ts of Being a Polite Guest

As a guest, it's important to remember that you're entering someone else's space, and being a polite guest can make all the difference. Being a polite guest is all about displaying good manners and etiquette. When invited to someone's home or event, it is essential to show respect and gratitude towards the host. Good manners dictate that guests should be punctual, dressed appropriately, and bring a small token of appreciation, such as a bouquet of flowers. Etiquette comes into play when it's time to interact with other guests and the host. It's important to make introductions, engage in polite conversation, and be mindful of the space and belongings of the host. Overall, being a polite guest is a crucial aspect of displaying good manners and etiquette in social situations.

Whether it's a dinner party, a weekend stay, or even just a quick visit, there are certain rules of etiquette that should be followed to ensure a positive experience for both you and your host. So, how do you become a polite guest? Let's take a look.

First and foremost, always RSVP as soon as possible. This is especially important for events such as weddings or formal dinners where the host needs to know the exact number of guests attending. A quick response shows that you appreciate the invitation and are excited to attend. If for some reason you can't attend, be sure to let the host know as soon as possible.

When it comes to arriving at your host's home, be punctual. Showing up too early or too late can be a major inconvenience for your host, so try to arrive at the designated time. If you're running late, let your host know as soon as possible.

Once you're inside, greet your host and any other guests with a warm smile and a handshake or hug. It's also a good idea to bring a small gift such as a box of chocolates. This shows your appreciation for the invitation and helps to set a positive tone for the evening.

When it's time to eat, wait for your host to take their seat before you sit down. It's also good manners to wait until everyone has been served before you start eating. And while it's tempting to dive in and enjoy the food, be sure to pace yourself and take small bites. You don't want to be the guest who finishes their meal in record time!

During the meal, engage in polite conversation with your host and fellow guests. Avoid controversial topics such as politics and religion, and instead stick to light and friendly topics such as travel or hobbies. And if you happen to spill or drop something, don't make a big deal out of it. Simply apologize and move on.

When it's time to leave, be sure to thank your host for their hospitality and let them know that you had a great time. It's also a good idea to offer to help with any clean-up or packing away any leftovers. And once you're outside, be sure to send a quick text or email thanking your host again for the lovely evening. Thank-you notes and other expressions of gratitude as well are classy and appropriate things to do.

Of course, these are just a few tips for being a polite guest. Here are some other Do's and Don'ts that will help make you the ideal guest:

Do's:

Do sit up straight and keep your elbows off the table.

Do wait for everyone to be served before you start eating.

Do use utensils properly, such as holding your knife and fork correctly and using them to cut and eat food.

Do hold the stem of a wine glass

Do use a napkin to dab your mouth or wipe your hands.

Do pass dishes around the table counterclockwise.

Do say "please" and "thank you" when asking for or receiving something.

Do chew with your mouth closed.

Do take small bites and eat slowly.

Do use appropriate conversation topics and avoid controversial or sensitive topics.

Do offer to help clear the table or wash dishes if you are a guest.

Don'ts

Don't blow your nose into a cloth napkin (either at someone's home or at a restaurant-it's gross!!)

Don't slouch or lean back in your chair.

Don't start eating until everyone is seated and served.

Don't talk with food in your mouth.

Don't reach across the table for something, ask for it to be passed.

Don't make loud noises when chewing or slurping.

Don't play with utensils or other objects on the table.

Don't use your phone or other electronic devices at the table.

Don't take excessively large bites or shovel food into your mouth.

Don't talk with your mouth full.

Don't push food onto someone else's plate or take food from someone else's plate without permission.

Don't demonstrate common guest faux pas: overstaying your welcome, being overly critical, etc.

The key is to be respectful and courteous at all times, and to show your appreciation for the invitation. With a little bit of effort, you can ensure that your next visit as a guest is a memorable and enjoyable one for both you and your host.

***

Navigating Tricky Situations With Grace and Poise

Navigating tricky situations with grace and poise can be a daunting task for anyone. Whether it's dealing with a difficult co-worker or handling an awkward social encounter, it's important to maintain a level of composure and professionalism. This is where good manners and etiquette come into play. By understanding how to handle these situations with grace and poise, we not only protect ourselves from embarrassing moments, but we also show respect and consideration for those around us.

One of the keys to navigating tricky situations is to always be prepared. This means anticipating potential challenges and having a plan in place for how to handle them. For example, if you're attending a party where you know there will be someone you don't get along with, consider strategizing ahead of time on how to avoid any uncomfortable interactions. This could mean arriving early and leaving before the person arrives, or positioning yourself in a different part of the room to avoid contact.

Another important aspect of navigating tricky situations is to always remain calm and composed. It can be tempting to react emotionally in these situations, but this often only makes things worse. Instead, take a deep breath, assess the situation, and respond in a calm and collected manner. This not only shows that you are in control, but it also sets the tone for those around you.

One common tricky situation is dealing with a rude or difficult person. In these situations, it's important to remember that you cannot control other people's behavior, but you can control your own. Instead of engaging in an argument or escalating the situation, try to remain polite and professional. This not only de-escalates the situation, but it also shows that you are the bigger person.

Another tricky situation that often arises is how to handle uncomfortable conversations. Whether it's discussing politics or dealing with a personal conflict, it's important to approach these conversations with sensitivity and respect. Avoid making assumptions, listen carefully to the other person's perspective, and respond in a calm and thoughtful manner. Remember, it's okay to agree to disagree, and sometimes the best course of action is to simply change the subject.

With tricky situations in the workplace, it's important to maintain a level of professionalism and respect for your colleagues. This means avoiding gossip, refraining from speaking negatively about others, and always keeping confidential information private. Additionally, it's important to be mindful of cultural and social differences, as what may be appropriate in one situation may not be in another.

Navigating tricky situations also means being mindful of your own behavior and how it may be perceived by others. This includes being punctual, dressing appropriately for the occasion, and avoiding behaviors that may be considered rude or offensive. For example, talking loudly on the phone or chewing with your mouth open can be seen as disrespectful and may make others uncomfortable.

A very common tricky situation that we all have faced is: What to do if you forget someone's name in a social situation? Forgetting someone's name in a social situation can be embarrassing, but it happens to everyone. Here are some tips on what to do:

- Ask for their name again: If it's appropriate, simply ask the person for their name again. They may not even realize you've forgotten.

- Introduce someone else: If you're with a friend or colleague, introduce them to the person whose name you've forgotten. This can prompt the person to introduce themselves again.

- Be honest: If you're really struggling to remember the person's name, be honest and apologize. They may appreciate your honesty and offer a reminder.

- Look for visual cues: Sometimes a person's name is linked to a visual cue, such as their job or where you met them. Use these cues to help jog your memory.

- Use context clues: Think about the context in which you met the person and what you talked about. This can help you remember their name.

Whatever you do, don't try to fake it by avoiding using their name or calling them by the wrong name. It's better to be honest and address the situation than to appear rude or insincere.

Ultimately, navigating tricky situations with grace and poise is about showing respect and consideration for those around you. By being prepared, remaining calm and composed, and approaching difficult situations with sensitivity and professionalism, we can not only protect ourselves from embarrassment, but also create a more positive and harmonious environment for everyone. Good manners and etiquette play a crucial role in this process, as they provide a framework for how we should behave in different social and professional settings.

Dealing with personal hygiene and health issues in public can be a sensitive topic. While it's important to maintain good personal hygiene for ourselves and those around us, it can be challenging to address issues that arise in public spaces without causing discomfort or offense. However, there are some tips and techniques that can help us navigate these situations with grace and poise.

One way to handle personal hygiene and health issues in public is to be discreet. If you need to take care of something like bad breath or body odor, try to step away from others and address it as privately as possible. This could mean excusing yourself to the restroom to freshen up, or discreetly applying deodorant or breath mints in a way that doesn't draw attention to yourself.

Another important consideration when dealing with personal hygiene and health issues in public is to be sensitive to others. If you notice that someone else is struggling with a hygiene issue, it's important to approach the situation with empathy and understanding. Avoid making assumptions or judgments, and instead offer assistance in a respectful and compassionate way.

In situations where you need to address someone else's hygiene or health issue, it's important to do so in a way that is tactful and respectful. For example, if someone has bad breath, you could offer them a mint or gum without drawing attention to the issue. Similarly, if someone is coughing or sneezing, you could offer them a tissue or hand sanitizer in a non-judgmental way.

It's also important to be prepared for unexpected hygiene or health issues that may arise in public. This could mean carrying a small hygiene kit with items like hand sanitizer, tissues, and breath mints, or having a discreet conversation with a friend or family member who is struggling with a personal hygiene issue.

Ultimately, the key to handling personal hygiene and health issues in public is to approach the situation with sensitivity and respect for both yourself and others. By being discreet, empathetic, and tactful, we can navigate these tricky situations with grace and poise, while also maintaining good personal hygiene and health for ourselves and those around us.

An overlooked, yet very important, tricky situation many of us may encounter is how to respectfully and tactfully decline an invitation to somewhere or to do something. Declining invitations gracefully is an important part of good manners and etiquette. While it can be uncomfortable to say no, it is better to be honest and polite than to make false promises or create expectations that you cannot meet.

Here are some tips for declining invitations with grace:

1. **Thank the person for the invitation.** Begin by expressing your gratitude for the invitation and the effort that the host has put into planning the event. A simple "Thank you so much for inviting me" can go a long way.

2. **Be honest but tactful.** If you cannot attend the event, it is best to be honest about the reason why. However, it is important to be tactful and avoid hurting the host's feelings. For example, instead of saying "I don't want to come," you can say something like "Unfortunately, I won't be able to make it this time."

3. **Offer an alternative**. If you cannot attend the event, but

would still like to spend time with the host, suggest an alternative date or activity that you can both enjoy. This shows that you value the person and the relationship.

4. **Don't over-explain**. While it is important to be honest, there is no need to go into great detail about why you cannot attend the event. Keep your explanation brief and to the point.

5. **Apologize sincerely.** If you are declining an invitation at the last minute or after having accepted it, apologize sincerely for any inconvenience you may have caused. Offer a sincere apology and let the host know that you appreciate the effort that went into planning the event.

6. **Send a gift or note:**. If you cannot attend the event, consider sending a small gift or a note to show that you are thinking of the host. This is a thoughtful gesture that can help to maintain the relationship.

Declining invitations with grace is an important part of good manners and etiquette. By being honest, tactful, and considerate, you can maintain positive relationships and avoid hurting others' feelings. Remember to thank the host for the invitation, offer an alternative, and apologize sincerely if necessary.

Navigating tricky and uncomfortable situations as a guest can be a daunting task, especially when trying to maintain a positive relationship with your host. While social etiquette and common sense can go a long way, there are still situations that can catch even the most seasoned guest off guard. Below is a Q&A section where we will explore some common and rare scenarios that can arise as a guest and offer advice on how to handle them with grace and ease. Whether you're attending a dinner party, staying overnight at someone's home, or attending a formal event, these tips and tricks will help you navigate any situation with confidence and ease. So, let's dive in and tackle those uncomfortable situations head-on!

What should I do if I accidentally spill wine on someone's expensive rug?

Apologize immediately and offer to have the rug professionally cleaned or pay for the cleaning cost. Do not try to clean it yourself or offer to replace it without consulting with the owner first.

What if I accidentally break something at someone's home?

Immediately let the host know and apologize. Offer to pay for the broken item. If it's a sentimental item, offer to have it repaired or replaced with something of equal or greater value.

What if I accidentally wear the same outfit as someone else to an event?

Laugh it off and don't make a big deal out of it. Compliment the other person on their style and try to differentiate yourself by adding accessories or styling your outfit differently.

What if I accidentally let out a loud burp or flatulence in public?

Beg your pardon quickly and discreetly, if possible. Excuse yourself to the restroom or to a private area if necessary. Try not to draw attention to the incident or make a joke out of it.

What if I accidentally insult someone unintentionally?

Ask for forgiveness immediately and sincerely. Explain that you didn't mean to offend them and ask if there is anything you can do to make amends. Try to learn from the mistake and be more mindful of your words and actions in the future.

What should someone do if they get sick attending a get together at someone's home?

If someone gets sick attending a get-together at someone's home, the first thing they should do is excuse themselves from the gathering and find a private area to recover. It is important to inform the host about their condition as soon as possible, either directly or through a trusted friend or family member. It is also a good idea for the sick person to apologize for any inconvenience or disruption they may have caused and to offer to make it up to the host at a later time. If necessary, the sick person should arrange for someone to take them home or seek medical attention. Finally, it is important for the sick person to follow up with the host after the event to express their gratitude and offer any further apologies or help as necessary.

If a person and their partner are invited to spend the night at someone's home, is it ok to have sex?

It is impolite and inappropriate to engage in sexual activities when staying as a guest in someone else's home. Doing so can make the hosts uncomfortable and may ruin the guest-host relationship. It's important to respect the boundaries and privacy of the hosts and maintain good manners and etiquette. If the guest and their partner wish to engage in sexual activities, they should make other arrangements, such as booking a hotel room.

What should someone do if they absolutely hate the meal that is being served when attending as a guest at someone's home?

If someone hates the meal being served while attending as a guest at someone's home, they should still show gratitude and manners by complimenting the host's efforts and attempting to eat as much as possible. They can also politely decline any seconds and focus on the other aspects of the gathering, such as the conversation and company. It's also important to remember that cultural differences in cuisine may exist, and what may be unusual or unappetizing to one person may be considered a delicacy or tradition to another.

What is the appropriate way to deal with an accidental toilet clogging in someone else's bathroom?

Accidentally clogging someone's toilet can be humiliating, but it's important to handle the situation with grace and consideration for the host. Here are some steps to follow:

1. Try to fix the problem yourself. Use a plunger or a toilet brush to see if you can unclog the toilet. If this doesn't work, move on to the next step.

2. Alert the host. Let them know what has happened and apologize for the inconvenience. Offer to help in any way you can, such as finding a plumber or cleaning up any water that has overflowed.

3. Take responsibility for any damages. If the toilet ends up needing repairs, offer to pay for them or to help cover the cost.

4. Be gracious and understanding. Accidents happen, and the host will appreciate your honesty and willingness to help. Offer to make it up to them somehow, such as inviting them over for dinner or sending them a thoughtful gift.

Remember, the most important thing is to handle the situation with kindness and respect.

Chapter Seven

Making Manners and Etiquette Your Own

Welcome to the final portion of this book: making manners and etiquette your own. By now, you have learned about everything from basic manners to formal dining, from being a great guest to hosting a successful event. But, you may still be wondering how to make all of these tips and guidelines your own. That's where this section comes in - how to personalize all of this information to make it work for you.

It's important to remember that manners and etiquette are not one-size-fits-all. What works for one person or situation may not work for another. However, the key to making manners and etiquette your own is to understand the underlying principles and adapt them to your unique personality and style.

For example, let's say you're an outgoing and gregarious person who loves to talk and make new friends. You may find that some of the traditional rules of small talk and conversation don't work for you. That's okay! You can still apply the principle of being respectful and attentive to the person you're talking to, while finding ways to make the conversation more natural and authentic to your own style.

Similarly, if you're a more reserved person, you may find some of the traditional rules of hosting or attending events overwhelming. However, you can still apply the principles of being gracious, welcoming, and attentive to your guests, while finding ways to make the event more comfortable and enjoyable for you.

The key to personalizing manners and etiquette is to make them your own without sacrificing the fundamental principles of respect, consideration, and kindness. That means understanding the context and expectations of a particular situation, while also staying true to your own personality and style.

So, how can you go about personalizing manners and etiquette? Here are a few tips to get you started:

- Reflect on your personal style and preferences. Think about what makes you feel comfortable and confident, and how you can incorporate that into your approach to manners and etiquette.

- Understand the context of the situation. Every situation is different, so take the time to understand the expectations and norms before adapting them to your own style.

- Be flexible and adaptable. Don't be afraid to try new things and experiment with different approaches. You may find that some things work better for you than others.

- Practice, practice, practice. The more you practice good manners and etiquette, the more natural they will become.

Remember, manners and etiquette are not about being perfect or following a strict set of rules. They're about showing respect, consideration, and kindness to others, while also staying true to yourself. When we treat others with respect and kindness, we show that we value them and their feelings. This can lead to stronger connections and more positive interactions.

Additionally, when we are knowledgeable and confident in our manners and etiquette, we feel more comfortable and at ease in social situations. This confidence can help us make a positive impression on others, leading to opportunities and success in both personal and professional settings.

Finally, good manners and etiquette are a reflection of our character and values. By demonstrating respect, kindness, and consideration for others, we show that we are trustworthy and dependable, which can further enhance our relationships and reputation. By personalizing these principles, you can make them work for you in any situation.

So, go forth and be your best, most authentic self, and always remember to mind your manners!

Chapter Eight

Chivalry (It's not just for Knights anymore)

Ah, chivalry - the code of conduct that has been around for centuries and has evolved with time. From knights in shining armor to modern-day gentlemen, the principles of chivalry have remained relevant, albeit with some adaptations to suit contemporary society.

The origins of chivalry can be traced back to the Middle Ages, where knights were expected to follow certain rules and practices. These included qualities like bravery, honor, loyalty, and generosity, which were deemed essential to the well-being of society. Knights were also expected to have a high level of education and skill, from swordsmanship to poetry, to impress their noblewomen.

As time went on, chivalry became more of a lifestyle and an ideal to strive for, rather than a code of conduct for knights. Chivalry now encompasses a range of behaviors that are seen as gentlemanly and respectful, not just towards women, but towards everyone.

One of the main benefits of chivalry is the impact it can have on building relationships. Being chivalrous involves showing consideration and respect for others, which can make people feel valued and appreciated. When you go out of your way to be kind and thoughtful, it can go a long way in forming strong bonds with others.

Chivalry can also help you gain respect from those around you. When you demonstrate qualities like honesty, integrity, and humility, you can earn the admiration and respect of your peers and colleagues. These qualities are especially important in professional settings, where being a respected and trustworthy individual can open up doors to new opportunities.

Another benefit of chivalry is the boost in confidence it can provide. When you conduct yourself in a respectful and courteous manner, it can give you a sense of self-assurance and poise. This can be especially helpful in social situations, where nerves and anxiety can often get the better of us. Knowing that you are conducting yourself in a manner that aligns with your values can give you the confidence to navigate any situation with grace and ease.

Chivalry has always been closely tied to manners and etiquette, as it embodies the ideal of a gentleman who is respectful, courteous, and considerate towards others. In the past, chivalry was a code of conduct followed by knights and nobles, emphasizing virtues such as honor, loyalty, bravery, and generosity. It included rules for behavior towards women, such as opening doors for them, offering to carry heavy items, and standing up when they entered a room. These actions were seen as a way of showing respect and protection towards women.

Today, while some aspects of chivalry may be seen as outdated or even sexist, the core values of respect and consideration towards others remain relevant. Many of the actions associated with chivalry, such as holding doors open for others, offering a helping hand, and showing kindness and consideration towards others, are still seen as good manners and are appreciated by both men and women. By embodying these values in our daily lives, we can show respect for others, build stronger relationships, and create a more courteous and considerate society.

In this section of the book, we will explore the meaning of chivalry and how it can be applied in our modern lives. We will delve into the key principles of chivalry, including respect, courtesy, and honor, and explore how they can be put into practice in a variety of situations. Whether it's in the workplace, social settings, or personal relationships, chivalry can be a powerful tool for building strong connections, earning respect, and boosting confidence. So let's strap on our armor and embark on this journey of chivalry together!

***

Chivalry Viewed Through a Modern Lens

For generations, parents have passed down the ideals of chivalry to their children. These teachings aim to instill respect, honor, and decency towards others, particularly women. From the late 19th century to the mid-20th century, chivalry was a common theme in parenting books, advice columns, and popular culture.

There are many examples of chivalry in movies from the first half of the 20th century that taught men how to treat and act around women. One of the most famous examples is the 1939 film "Gone with the Wind," in which Rhett Butler (played by Clark Gable) displays chivalrous behavior towards Scarlett O'Hara (played by Vivien Leigh) by opening doors for her, helping her with her coat, and generally treating her with respect and courtesy. Another example is the 1942 film "Casablanca," in which Rick Blaine (played by Humphrey Bogart) displays chivalrous behavior towards Ilsa Lund (played by Ingrid Bergman) by protecting her and helping her escape danger. Other examples can be found in films such as "It Happened One Night" (1934), "The Philadelphia Story" (1940), and "An Affair to Remember" (1957), in which male characters display chivalrous behavior towards their female counterparts. These films not only entertained audiences but also provided them with examples of how men should behave towards women in a respectful and courteous manner.

Parents encouraged their sons to be polite, courteous, and considerate towards women. They were taught to open doors, pull out chairs, and carry heavy loads for women. They were also encouraged to protect and defend women in distress.

Chivalry was also taught to young women, who were expected to behave in a ladylike manner, including being modest, gracious, and demure. They were encouraged to accept gentlemanly gestures from men, such as holding open doors and offering to carry packages.

While some aspects of chivalry may seem outdated today, the core principles of respect and consideration for others remain relevant. Parents continue to pass down these values to their children, adapting them to modern times.

In today's world, the teachings of chivalry have evolved to include respect and consideration for people of all genders and backgrounds. These values have become more inclusive and reflect the changing roles of men and women in society.

***

How Ideas of Masculinity and Femininity Have Changed Over Time

The ideas of masculinity and femininity have evolved significantly over time. In the past, there were strict gender roles that dictated how men and women should behave, dress, and even think. Men were expected to be strong, assertive, and in control, while women were expected to be nurturing, submissive, and obedient. These gender roles were often reinforced by social norms, religious beliefs, and cultural traditions.

However, over the past century, there has been a gradual shift away from these traditional gender roles. This shift was influenced by a variety of factors, including the rise of feminism, changes in the workplace, and the spread of more progressive and inclusive ideas about gender and sexuality.

Today, there is a growing recognition that gender is not simply a binary choice between male and female, but rather a complex and fluid spectrum that includes people of all genders and identities. Many people now reject traditional gender roles and embrace a more gender-neutral approach to life, where individuals are free to express themselves however they choose, without fear of judgment or discrimination.

Overall, the evolution of ideas of masculinity and femininity has been marked by a gradual expansion of what it means to be a man or a woman, and a greater acceptance of diverse gender identities and expressions. While there is still much work to be done to achieve full gender equality, the progress that has been made so far is a testament to the power of social change and the human capacity for growth and transformation.

***

Chivalry May Be Seen As Outdated or Even Sexist

Chivalry, as a code of conduct for knights in medieval times, emphasized virtues such as honor, courage, loyalty, and gallantry toward women. Over time, this code of conduct evolved into a set of social norms that became associated with male behavior toward women, including acts such as holding doors open, paying for dates, and giving up seats on public transport. While these acts may have been intended as acts of respect and consideration, they can be seen as outdated and sexist in today's society.

The origins of modern chivalry can be traced back to the Victorian era, where strict gender roles and societal expectations placed women in a subservient position to men. Men were expected to be the providers and protectors, while women were expected to be passive and demure. These expectations were reinforced by popular culture, including movies, literature, and advertising, which depicted women as helpless and in need of male protection.

As women's rights movements gained traction in the 20th century, these traditional gender roles began to be challenged. Women began to demand equality and respect, and the idea of chivalry as a form of benevolent sexism began to be questioned. Many women found the idea of being treated as delicate and in need of protection to be patronizing and offensive, and preferred to be treated as equals.

Today, while some women still appreciate acts of chivalry, many others find them unnecessary or even insulting. They feel that these acts imply that women are weak and unable to take care of themselves, and that men are obligated to provide for and protect them. In addition, some women find that being treated differently because of their gender creates a sense of discomfort or even hostility.

While chivalry may have had its roots in noble ideals of honor and respect, it has evolved into a set of gendered social norms that can be seen as outdated and even offensive. As society continues to evolve and gender roles become more fluid, it is important to recognize that treating women with respect and consideration does not have to be tied to outdated notions of chivalry. Rather, it is simply a matter of treating all people with kindness, respect, and dignity, regardless of gender.

Chapter Nine

The Return of Chivalry: Making A Case

In a world where gender roles and traditional values are constantly being challenged, the concept of chivalry may seem antiquated and irrelevant. Some may even argue that it is sexist and promotes outdated notions of gender roles. However, I believe that there is still a place for chivalry in the 21st century.

Chivalry is not just about opening doors or offering a coat to a lady on a cold evening. It is about embodying a set of values and ideals that go beyond simple acts of kindness. It is about showing respect, honor, and kindness towards others, regardless of gender or any other characteristic.

In many ways, chivalry is about being a decent human being. It means treating others with dignity and respect, and going out of your way to make others feel valued and appreciated. It means being selfless, putting others before yourself, and striving to make the world a better place.

Some may argue that chivalry reinforces gender stereotypes and is therefore inherently sexist. However, I believe that this is a misunderstanding of what chivalry truly represents. Chivalry is not about subjugating women or treating them as inferior. Rather, it is about recognizing and appreciating the unique qualities and strengths of each gender, and working together to create a more harmonious society.

In fact, many women today still appreciate chivalrous gestures, such as opening doors or offering to carry heavy items. These acts of kindness and consideration are not seen as demeaning or patronizing, but rather as a sign of respect and appreciation.

Furthermore, chivalry can also play a role in creating more positive and healthy relationships. By embodying the values of chivalry, both men and women can create a more loving, supportive, and respectful environment for themselves and those around them.

Ultimately, chivalry is not about following a set of rigid rules or guidelines. Rather, it is about embodying a set of values and ideals that promote kindness, respect, and selflessness. By embracing these values and making them a part of our daily lives, we can create a better, more harmonious world for everyone.

***

Redefining What Chivalry Is

Chivalry, in its traditional sense, has been criticized for being exclusive and sexist. However, it is possible to redefine chivalry to fit a more diverse and inclusive world.

One way to do this is to focus on the core values of chivalry - respect, kindness, and honor - and apply them to all individuals, regardless of gender or background. It is important to recognize that everyone deserves to be treated with respect and kindness, regardless of their gender, race, sexuality, or any other characteristic.

Another way to redefine chivalry is to encourage people to be mindful of their actions and the impact they have on others. This includes being aware of power dynamics and taking steps to ensure that everyone feels comfortable and safe. For example, if someone notices that a person in a group is being talked over or ignored, they can step in and ensure that their voice is heard.

It is also important to recognize that chivalry is not just about how men should treat women. It is about how everyone should treat each other. This means that women can also practice chivalry by treating others with respect and kindness.

In addition, redefining chivalry can involve challenging traditional gender roles and expectations. This means encouraging men to be more emotionally expressive and vulnerable, and encouraging women to take on leadership roles and assert themselves. By challenging these norms, we can create a more equitable and inclusive society.

Overall, redefining chivalry to fit a more diverse and inclusive world involves focusing on the core values of respect, kindness, and honor, being mindful of power dynamics, recognizing that chivalry is not just about men and women, and challenging traditional gender roles and expectations.

***

Chivalry and the Modern Woman

Picture this: a modern woman, capable and strong, independent and self-sufficient, navigating through the world with grace and confidence. Is chivalry something that has a place in her life? Can it coexist with her empowered and self-determined sense of self? The answer is yes, but with a twist.

In the modern world, we can reimagine the concept of chivalry to suit women and their relationships with others. Women can benefit from practicing chivalry in their daily lives. Holding doors open, offering to carry heavy objects, and showing basic courtesy and respect to others are all acts of chivalry that can make a difference in people's lives. It's about being aware of others and doing small things that can make their day a little easier or more pleasant.

In a world that can sometimes feel harsh and unforgiving, chivalry can be a way to counteract negativity and promote kindness. By practicing chivalry, women can set an example for others and create a ripple effect of positivity in their communities.

But what about the concerns that chivalry might perpetuate traditional gender roles and stereotypes? This is a valid question, and it's important to recognize that chivalry can be redefined to fit a more modern understanding of gender and sexuality. It's not about men serving women or women being submissive to men, but rather about treating everyone with dignity and respect, regardless of gender.

As times change and societal norms evolve, so too must our understanding and practice of chivalry. The days of knights in shining armor and courtly love may be long gone, but the core principles of chivalry can still have a place in our modern world. While chivalry was traditionally associated with men demonstrating honor and respect towards women, in today's society it is important to recognize and embrace the fact that chivalry is not limited to gender roles. Women can demonstrate chivalry towards men and other women, and men can do the same towards women and other men.

***

Chivalry and the LGBTQ+ Community

Chivalry is often associated with traditional gender roles and heterosexual relationships, but it doesn't have to be limited to those contexts. In recent years, there has been a growing recognition of the importance of inclusivity and diversity in chivalric practices, especially with regards to the LGBTQ+ community. While some may argue that chivalry is a relic of the past, its principles of respect, honor, and compassion are still relevant and valuable in modern society.

For members of the LGBTQ+ community, chivalry can take on new meanings and expressions that reflect their unique experiences and identities. From simple acts of kindness to grand gestures of love, chivalry can be a way for LGBTQ+ individuals to express their pride, respect, and support for one another. In this context, chivalry can help to foster a sense of community, acceptance, and belonging.

At the same time, chivalry can also be a means of bridging divides between LGBTQ+ individuals and those outside the community. By demonstrating chivalric behavior towards those who may not share the same gender identity or sexual orientation, LGBTQ+ individuals can challenge stereotypes and promote understanding and empathy. By embodying the principles of chivalry in their daily interactions, they can help to break down barriers and create a more inclusive and compassionate society.

In today's world, it's important to recognize and acknowledge the diverse range of gender identities and expressions that exist. This includes those who identify as non-binary or transgender and may prefer to use pronouns other than the traditional he/him or she/her.

As a chivalrous individual, it's important to respect someone's gender identity and use the appropriate pronouns when addressing them. This may require a bit of education and effort on your part, but it shows that you value and honor that person's identity.

Using the correct pronouns is a simple yet powerful way to demonstrate chivalry and respect towards others. It shows that you are willing to meet people where they are and honor their individuality. So whether it's using they/them, ze/zir, or any other pronoun, taking the time to learn and use someone's preferred pronouns is an important aspect of modern chivalry.

Of course, there are unique challenges and considerations that come with practicing chivalry in the LGBTQ+ community. For example, some traditional expressions of chivalry may not be appropriate or desirable for all individuals, depending on their personal preferences and experiences. It is also important to recognize the diversity and complexity of the LGBTQ+ community, and to approach chivalric practices with sensitivity and respect for different identities, cultures, and histories.

Ultimately, chivalry in the LGBTQ+ community is about creating a culture of kindness, respect, and dignity, regardless of gender identity or sexual orientation. It is about celebrating differences and embracing diversity, while also upholding the timeless values of honor, bravery, and compassion. By reimagining chivalry in this way, we can create a more inclusive and equitable society that benefits us all.

***

Practicing Chivalry In Daily Life

Practicing chivalry in daily life may seem like a daunting task, but it doesn't have to be. There are countless small ways to incorporate chivalry into your daily routine that can make a big difference in how you interact with others. Some examples include holding the door open for someone, offering to carry a heavy load, saying "please" and "thank you" with sincerity, and giving compliments that are not solely based on appearance.

In addition to these simple gestures, it's important to make a conscious effort to treat others with kindness and respect, even in the face of conflict or disagreement. This means practicing active listening, being mindful of other people's feelings, and avoiding judgment or assumptions based on superficial characteristics. By practicing chivalry in these ways, like the ones listed below, we can create a more courteous and considerate society, one small act of kindness at a time.

***

Chivalrous Acts You Can Do For Your Partner

Chivalry isn't dead! In fact, it's more alive than ever! Whether you're dating, engaged, or in a long-term relationship, there are plenty of chivalrous acts you can do for your significant other to make them feel valued and appreciated. From opening doors to cooking dinner, these small gestures can go a long way in strengthening your relationship and making your partner feel loved. So, let's explore some chivalrous acts you can do for your partner!

*****Please note that in the following examples, I am using "they" as a gender-neutral pronoun to refer to an individual, rather than using "he" or "she".*****

1. **They Keep Their Word.** shows a sense of honor and integrity. When someone makes a promise or commitment, they are essentially giving their word and implying that they will follow through on their commitment. By keeping their word, they demonstrate they are reliable, trustworthy, and respectful of others' time and expectations.

2. **They Check To See You Got Home Safely.** is a simple act of caring and concern, which is why it can be considered an act of chivalry. When a person takes the time to ensure that their friend, loved one, or acquaintance made it home safely, they show they value that person's well-being and will take steps to protect it.

3. **They Open The Car Door, As Well As All Doors.** Opening doors for others, especially women, is a traditional act of chivalry. It shows respect and courtesy towards the person and can make them feel valued and cared for. By opening the car door or any door for someone, the chivalrous person is showing their willingness to put the other person's needs ahead of their own, even in small ways. It is a simple but effective way to make someone feel special and appreciated.

4. **They Text You During The Day.** Texting someone during the day is an act of chivalry because it shows that the person is thinking of the other person and cares about their well-being. It's a small gesture that can help maintain a connection and make the other person feel valued and appreciated.

5. **They Give You Their Undivided Attention.** Giving someone your undivided attention is an act of chivalry be-

cause it shows that you value and respect their presence and time. It requires setting aside distractions and focusing solely on the person in front of you, which can make them feel heard, understood, and appreciated. It also allows for deeper and more meaningful conversations and connections.

6. **They Plan Dates.** Planning dates can be an act of chivalry as it shows effort, thoughtfulness, and a desire to create a special experience for the person you're with. It can show your interest in getting to know them better and your willingness to take charge and make decisions that will make them feel appreciated and valued. By planning a date, you are creating a memorable experience and show that you care about making the other person happy.

7. **They're Open About Their Intentions.** Being open about his intentions is an act of chivalry because it shows honesty and respect. By clearly communicating his intentions, he avoids leading the other person on and allows them to make informed decisions about the relationship. This also helps to build trust and establishes a foundation for a healthy and respectful relationship.

8. **They Pay The Bill.** When a man pays for a date or a meal, it is often seen as a traditional act of chivalry. It shows that he values the woman's company and will invest in the relationship. However, it's important to note that this act of chivalry doesn't mean that the woman is incapable of paying or that the man is entitled to anything in return. It is simply a gesture of kindness and respect.

9. **They Walk You To Your Front Door.** Walking someone to their front door is an act of chivalry that shows respect and care for their safety. By accompanying them to their doorstep, they show they will ensure that they will arrive home safely, even if it means extending the date a little longer. It allows for a natural opportunity to say goodnight and express an interest in seeing them again.

10. **They Kiss You On The Forehead At The End of a Date.** Kissing someone on the forehead can be seen as a sign of respect, care, and protection. When a man kisses his date on the forehead at the end of a date, it is a gesture of chivalry that shows he values her as a person, not just as a romantic interest. It is a simple act that can leave a lasting impression of care and tenderness.

11. **They Give You Real Compliments.** Giving real compliments can be an act of chivalry because it shows that the person is paying attention to the other person and is genuinely interested in them. It also builds the other person's confidence and self-esteem, which is a sign of respect and admiration. When done sincerely and respectfully, giving compliments can strengthen the relationship and create a positive atmosphere of mutual appreciation and kindness.

12. **They Walk Closest To The Road.** When walking with a woman on the sidewalk, it is considered an act of chivalry for a man to walk closest to the road. This practice is rooted in the idea of protecting the woman from potential dangers, such as splashing from passing vehicles or being hit by a stray object. By walking closest to the road, the man takes on the

physical risk and shows his willingness to protect and care for his companion. It may seem like a small gesture, but it can make a woman feel valued and respected.

13. **They Let You Order First.** Allowing a woman to order first at a restaurant is an act of chivalry that shows respect and consideration. It shows that the man will defer to the woman's preferences and puts her comfort and desires first. It also reflects an understanding of traditional gender roles where men are expected to take care of and protect women.

14. **They Wait For You Before You Begin To Eat If His Food Arrives First**. Waiting for your partner to eat before you do is a small but significant gesture of consideration and respect. It shows that you value their presence and company, and you want to enjoy the meal together. By waiting, you acknowledge that you are equals, and that their needs and desires are just as important as yours. This act of chivalry is a way to show that you are thoughtful and attentive to your partner's needs and feelings.

15. **They Make Sure You're Having A Great Time.** Making sure your partner is having a great time is an act of chivalry because it shows that you care about their enjoyment and well-being. This could involve checking in on them throughout the night, making sure they have everything they need, and actively seeking out activities or experiences that you know they will enjoy. It demonstrates a level of consideration and thoughtfulness that can make a big difference in a relationship.

Chapter Ten

Conclusion

As we near the end of our journey through the world of manners, etiquette, and chivalry, it's important to remember that these practices are not simply a set of rules to follow, but rather a way of life. By embodying the principles of respect, kindness, and consideration for others, we can create a more harmonious and respectful society.

Here's a few additional rules that can help guide us towards being the best versions of ourselves.

1. You can make a big difference in someone's comfort level by offering your coat or jacket if they feel cold. Although it may seem like a small gesture, it can go a long way in showing your thoughtfulness and concern for their well-being.

2. Surprising your partner with small acts of kindness can go a long way in making them feel loved and appreciated. This can include leaving a thoughtful note on their pillow or even surprising them with their favorite cup of coffee in the morning.

Stop saying, "Ladies First.". Instead, use the term "Please,

3. after you." instead. It's a great way to be more inclusive and avoid misgendering someone. It allows for individuals to enter a door or pass through a space based on the order of arrival, rather than their gender. This minor change in language can make a big difference in creating a more welcoming and respectful environment for everyone.

4. Organize unique and personalized dates or activities that align with your partner's interests and tastes. This shows your attentiveness to their wants and needs.

5. Being attentive to the small things can make a big impact. Remembering their favorite food or music, or simply asking about their day and actively listening, shows that you value them as a unique individual.

6. Tip at least 20%. Your server works hard to ensure that you have an enjoyable dining experience, from taking your order to bringing out your food and drinks, and everything in between. In fact, servers often rely heavily on tips to make a living wage, as their base pay may be well below minimum wage.

7. Also, be kind to your server. Not being nice to your server says a lot about you, and none of it is good. It shows that you lack basic manners and respect for others. It screams entitlement and a lack of empathy. And let's not forget the most obvious one: it makes you look like a total jerk. So, if you want to be seen as a decent human being, treat your server with kindness and respect.

8. Don't post pictures of other people on social media without

asking permission first is generally not considered polite or respectful because it violates their privacy and personal space. People have the right to control their own image and how it is shared online, as well as you can be potentially exposing them to unwanted attention or even danger.

9. Get into the habit of not saying yes when you really mean no. It can lead to miscommunication and confusion. Saying yes when you really want to say no can also result in feelings of resentment, stress, and even anger towards the person or situation. It's important to be honest with yourself and with others about your wants and needs in order to maintain healthy relationships and boundaries. Saying no when you mean no can be difficult, but it is ultimately more respectful and beneficial for everyone involved.

10. Please clean up your dog's mess. This is not only a matter of common courtesy, it's also about hygiene, and a way to show consideration for others who may use the same space.

11. Cover your cough or sneeze. We live in a post-Covid-19 world. This is not only good manners, but potentially life-saving.

12. Placing your napkin on your lap is typically done when sitting down to eat a meal, as it provides a convenient and accessible place to wipe your mouth or hands while dining. However, putting your napkin next to your plate, not on it, should be done when you finish eating or need to step away from the table temporarily, as it signals to the server that you are not finished with your meal and will be returning. Addi-

tionally, placing your napkin next to your plate is considered a more formal and polite way to indicate that you are done eating, while placing it on your lap is seen as more casual.

13. On the subject of napkins, here's another helpful rule: Proper placement of napkins. When it comes to using a napkin in a restaurant versus at someone's home, there are some subtle differences to keep in mind. In a restaurant, it's generally best to place the napkin in your lap before as soon as you sit down. At someone's home, you can usually place your napkin on your lap as soon as the host sits down. Doing it before your host sits down may send a message that you are rushing them.

14. Now listen up, folks. Unless you're a walking, talking public service announcement, please keep your phone calls to yourself. That means no shouting into your phone on the bus, no playing your voicemails on speaker in the park, and definitely no FaceTiming while walking down a sidewalk. Remember, you don't want to be that person that everyone gives the stink eye to. Remember, the other person may think their conversation with you in private and not being broadcast to strangers in earshot."

15. Which brings us to this: Let others know when they're on speakerphone. See #12 for the reasons why. If I am calling you to help me, for example, "bury the body", I would prefer to keep it on the down low. Wink wink. The world, and the "5-0" don't need to hear our plans. Capeesh?

16. When squeezing a lemon or lime slice into your drink, shield

it when squeezing it so it doesn't make a mess or get on someone. (On a side note: I have worked in food and beverage for a long time. NEVER put a lemon or lime slice into your drink when you are at a bar or restaurant. No one washes the rind, which means whatever bacteria or dirt that is on it, is now mixed in with your iced tea or martini.)

17. Please don't text or talk during a movie. Lit phone screens can be a distraction for some, and no talking or whispering during a movie annoys others who have also paid good money to watch and enjoy the film. Same goes for theatres, comedy clubs, concerts, etc.

18. When you are driving, use your turn signal, as well as letting someone who is trying to get into your lane to get in ahead of you. Better to be polite and safe, then endangering those on the road with you.

19. Returning your shopping cart to the designated corral instead of leaving it in the middle of the parking lot. It is not only a matter of basic consideration and respect for others, but it also shows that you are a responsible and conscientious member of society. Abandoning your cart in the middle of the lot is not only rude, but it can also cause damage to other vehicles, and can create a hazard for others trying to park or navigate the area. Plus, returning your cart to the corral is just a small act of kindness that can make a big difference in someone's day, like the person who has to collect and redistribute the carts. Remember, manners aren't just about being polite, they're about being a considerate and respectful human being.

20. If you are not buying the meal, don't order the most expensive item. It shows a lack of consideration for the person who is treating you to the meal and can come off as entitled or disrespectful. It's better to choose something moderately priced and show gratitude for the invitation instead of taking advantage of someone else's generosity. Remember, good manners are always in style!

21. You should accept other people's apologies. If someone is big enough to offer a sincere apology, you should be big enough to accept.

22. Whether you are walking down a sidewalk, walking in the mall, going up or down stairs, it's considered polite to keep to the right, allowing people to pass you on the left. If you need to stop for any reason, step to the side. And remember to not block any doorways or entrances.

23. Stop bringing wine as a gift to the host of a dinner at their home: Bringing a bottle of wine as a gift to the host of a dinner at their home may seem like a thoughtful gesture, but it can actually be quite problematic. While wine may be appreciated, it can also make the host feel obligated to use the wine during the meal, even if it doesn't complement the food being served. Additionally, the host may already have selected a specific wine to pair with the meal, making the gifted wine redundant. Instead of bringing wine, consider bringing a small, thoughtful gift that the host can enjoy at their leisure, like a scented candle or a box of chocolates.

***

Well, well, well, here we are at the end of this wonderful book on manners, etiquette, and chivalry. Can you believe it? We've covered so much ground, from the basics of opening doors to the intricacies of handling all sorts of social interactions and occasions. But before we say our final farewells, let's take a moment to recap the importance of manners and chivalry in today's society.

First and foremost, let's remember that manners are not just about knowing which fork to use or how to properly address someone in a formal setting. It's about showing respect and consideration for those around us, whether it be our partner, friends, family, or even strangers. It's about acknowledging the humanity and dignity of others and treating them with kindness and civility.

Chivalry, on the other hand, takes manners a step further. It's about not just showing respect and consideration, but actively seeking to protect and honor others, particularly those who may be vulnerable or in need of assistance. It's about embodying the qualities of courage, honor, and integrity, and using those qualities to lift up those around us.

Now, some may argue that chivalry is outdated or even sexist, but let's dispel that myth right now. Chivalry is not about men acting as the saviors of helpless women, or about perpetuating outdated gender roles. Rather, it's about all of us, regardless of gender or identity, striving to be the best versions of ourselves and treating others with the utmost respect and care.

Manners and chivalry may seem like old-fashioned concepts, but they are just as relevant today as they were in centuries past. In a world that can often be harsh and unforgiving, these small acts of kindness and respect can make all the difference in creating a more compassionate and empathetic society. So go forth and practice chivalry and manners in your daily life, and let's all strive to be the best versions of ourselves.